MW00786292

For Abdul, Layla and Eden

– Karima

For my parents Ibrahim and
Amineh, wish you were here
to see this

– Sivine

Sofra

LEBANESE
RECIPES
TO SHARE

KARIMA HAZIM CHATILA
& SIVINE TABBOUCH

quadrille

Contents

Love, Food, Culture and Community

I have loved food for as long as I can remember and, without a doubt, I inherited this love from my mother, Sivine – who I would watch dance around the kitchen humming while she cooked – and from her mother before her in a long heritage stretching back into my deep roots in Lebanon. For them, cooking was not a chore. Instead it was a marriage of two things: sharing of culture and nourishment.

My mother came to Australia at the age of eleven but her heart was always in Tripoli – the source of her pioneering, courageous and hospitable spirit. In Lebanon, food is meant to be plentiful and shared generously. And food served as a language in my family, a way to show love and nurture, a way to share family history and a way my mother instilled strong cultural values in her three daughters.

Every day, even though she went out to work, my mother only ever cooked traditional Lebanese food for me and my sisters and we would often be greeted with a pot of *tabikh* (a slow-cooked dish). As a family we would come together every other weekend and share a decadent array of Lebanese dishes, in good times and in sad ones too, over a spread Mum put together with so much care and attention. Gathering around food was our safe and restorative practice, a space rid of tension, hostility and prejudice and although words were not necessarily always communicated, the silence was full of gratitude and blessing. This is the meaning of *sofra*.

Sofra is a tribute to our families. It is a celebration of family history, of culture and the traditions that bind our families together and that have travelled not only across the world but through generations. The stories of our families are told through food, the spreads of dishes that connect us to our homeland and bring us together around the table each weekend. *Sofra* is an ode to our mothers, grandmothers and aunts, who would spend days cooking for their children and grandchildren. A typical Lebanese Sunday lunch is a spread that tells the story of the rich and diverse regions of Lebanon, the seasons and agriculture of each town and village and the unique traditions of its communities.

Apart from celebrating cultural and religious festivities like Eid and Christmas, these gatherings are a way of upholding family values, food being the bind. Hosting these lunches is a deliciously sacred obligation, a sign of respect and adoration, for grandparents in particular. Once invited, it is your *wajeb* (obligation) not only to respectfully accept the invitation, arrive with Lebanese sweets in hand and leave with a plate of leftovers, but to return the invitation in the future. At the gathering you are likely to encounter a family member or friend you may not have seen for a while, and you will extend the invitation to lunch, and so the cycle continues.

As Lebanese people, we are hospitable in every way, not just by habit but because it is part of our culture and traditions. Food is an ice breaker, and a way we have always welcomed family, neighbours, colleagues and peers and made them feel comfortable.

A Glance at Lebanese History

Lebanese migrants, such as my mother and father, have been arriving in Australia since the second half of the 19th century, risking the long and perilous journey. The majority settled in Sydney. In the 1890s, migration increased before slowing down dramatically with the introduction of the Immigration Restriction Act in 1901. When the chain migration policy was introduced after the Second World War, it was almost designed with the Lebanese spirit in mind. Friends or relatives of existing established families were granted entry to Australia provided they would be supported and assisted to settle by relatives or sponsors.

Growing up, I often heard stories of when the civil war broke out in Lebanon in 1975. It was then that my parents, with numerous other families, made the courageous decision to abandon their homes, families and communities in search of safety. Some were fortunate enough to have their own family and friends already in their adopted country. Those who did not, found no less a reception – from the affluent to those with only meagre resources – who welcomed the strangers into their homes, often for two years or more, regardless of religion or sect. How ironic when you consider that the civil war divided the Lebanese people on the lines of seemingly irreconcilable religious differences and that Lebanon's government is still divided along sectarian lines. Yet, these political divides played little part in the spirit of the Lebanese migrants.

The heart of this generous welcome was always food. Just as strongly now as then. Over the familiar aromas of the kitchens of childhood, tales of Lebanon – with its abundantly green villages and diverse food culture – were shared.

The Life Left Behind

Sivine: I was born in the city of Tripoli in the north of Lebanon, the second youngest in a family of nine boys and six girls. My parents founded a renowned sweet shop and we were well known in the community.

As a child, my days were filled with plenty of play and joy, life was simple and food was a central part of family life. With many mouths to feed, my mother was incredibly resourceful at building a village around her to create the nourishing meals we grew up enjoying. She sourced her ingredients in the souks, which were filled with men and women from the northern villages selling fresh milk, homemade cheese and mountain bread as well as fresh fruits and vegetables. She would call on neighbours, friends and family and have days where they would prepare labour-intensive dishes together, many hands making light work.

I always knew what my mother was making for dinner from the pot simmering on the stove and the ingredients she had laid out the night before. Whenever it didn't suit me, I would take myself off to our local butcher and request a freshly cooked *kafta* (spiced lamb mince) sandwich, and ask to put it on my father's tab. 'When will you start paying for your own food?' the older men teased. 'Don't you know who my father is?' I would yell back, running to my next destination, which was a hole in the wall selling *jallab*, a drink made of date molasses and rosewater poured over shaved ice, and generously topped with soaked pine nuts. The souk was a treasure chest, full of secret nooks and hidden vendors, bakeries, sweet shops and fresh produce. My parents' sweet shop was in this very souk, and my mother would send me there most mornings for steaming hot *haboub* (barley and chickpea porridge) for breakfast before school.

Emigrating to Australia

Sivine: On 23 September 1976, I arrived in Australia at the age of eleven, completely unaware of the magnitude of leaving my home in Lebanon. The final two weeks in Tripoli were chaos; my parents fought day and night, to the sound of machine gun fire and explosions as the civil war tore through the city. My father was convinced it would all be over soon and forbade my mother from leaving with the six children who were still at home. The thought of her sons parading through the streets armed with guns made my mother sick to her stomach. After five days outside the embassy begging for a protection visa, my mother was granted *laissez passes* to Australia for herself and her children.

I grieved for the life I loved in my home country. We felt like outsiders and struggled to comprehend our surroundings. Watching my mother's struggle broke my heart. This tall, confident woman in her black *abaya* (a loose outer garment), commanding every place she went, suddenly collapsed. Without her community around her, she lost her sense of self and identity. We would retreat each day around a simple meal and reminisce about our life in Tripoli. After six years, my father joined us and, although I was elated to see him, my heart broke again, for I knew that this meant our fate had been cemented. We were not returning to Lebanon.

Fostering Community

Sivine: My mother's efforts to settle in her new country grew more successful. She had an amazing ability to remember everyone's background and was a master at building connections and fostering a sense of community. As more Lebanese migrants arrived and brought new skills, the community began to flourish. I often accompanied my mother to our local shops and watched as she began to forge relationships. Soon the shelves were stacked with a wider range of produce, encouraging my mother to the kitchen to begin cooking again, not just for nourishment but for healing.

As the youngest daughter, I ended up in the kitchen with my mother not by choice, but so I would be allowed to go out with my friends if I helped her. At first my mother said little, but I could tell by the tone of her humming that she was grateful for my presence. What began as a chore soon became our joint activity, working with our hands as she told me about the life she had left behind.

Through cooking I got to really know my mother and as my heart broke for her sadness and struggles, I saw that her food was infused with so much compassion and intent, made with love and longing. Our life in Lebanon somehow remained alive with each dish and spread, and our meals became the foundations I took to my own family several years later. I wanted my family to enjoy the same meals I grew up eating as a way of sharing our heritage with my children.

Following the birth of my first born and several years of social work, I asked my mother how she had coped with motherhood, especially with fifteen children. She laughed and reminded me of the community she left behind. She had a village, women who lived close by, who would come together and prepare dishes while celebrating, comforting and consoling one another. Listening to my mother speak of her neighbours and friends and seeing the vital role they played in her life and wellbeing instilled a strong sense of community in me and food became my way of bringing people together.

My Memories of Childhood

By the time I was born, my parents had been in Australia for some years. I was raised and educated In Australia, although my cultural and culinary heritage were very much based in my parents' homeland. Mum insisted that we went to Arabic school on Sunday for eight years to learn Arabic, ignoring all our tantrums and refusals, and I will be forever indebted to her for that, because it was through language and food that I developed this deep love and connection to my Lebanese heritage, the shaping of my identity, and something I would come back searching for many years later.

My sharpest memories of childhood are centred around food, and it takes merely a sound or a scent to transport me back to those precious moments – many details lost but those of food still crystal clear.

We visited my grandparents' house frequently as children. I loved the large tall pots of *mahshi warak enab* (stuffed vine leaves) and *mahshi malfouf* (stuffed cabbage rolls) and bunches of *molokhia* (jute leaves) that were picked and dried in the sitting room, and the large *toot* (mulberry) tree that stood in their garden. While my parents worked, some school holidays were spent at my uncle's place, a treasure chest of food, as his wife Fadila loved to cook. Her kitchen was laced with jars of preserved olives and pickled vegetables, trays of *shanklish* (soft cheese) speckled with sun-dried chilli, pots of tall chillies and cherry tomatoes and a wild grape vine that wrapped around the balcony. Always curious, mesmerized by the electric colour, I once dipped my finger in some freshly crushed chillies to taste them – my tongue numb from the pain for days afterwards.

There were also annual trips to my dad's village in Lebanon, and I can still trace every corner of the kitchen at my grandmother's house, the dark stone pantry full of the year's *mouneh* (pantry staples), and the flat sheet on the roof drying figs, apricots and bulgur wheat.

The women in my family solved many of the world's problems around the kitchen table; it was the only way they knew how. Whether rolling and stuffing vine leaves, crushing olives or baking, we would retreat to the kitchen and discuss everyday matters while sipping cups of coffee as the matriarchal wisdom overflowed. No family is perfect and ours certainly wasn't, but our celebrations and gatherings were deeply layered, not just full of food, but infused with emotion, love, struggle and breakthrough. It was important these stories were communicated, and shared, for they are much more important than a recipe or a beautiful picture.

This tradition, although at times exhausting, was the only way we children of migrants were able to taste and experience the traditional Lebanese foods and spreads our grandparents and ancestors grew up eating. Sunday lunch also kept the Arabic language alive through conversations with our grandparents, even just the basics, both in the kitchen and around the table.

The Beginning of Sunday Kitchen

Once I started a family, cooking became the centre of my world. At the time I had only ever cooked alongside my mother, Sivine, in a supporting role. So I spent a long time on the phone with Mum trying to perfect traditional stews for my hungry family. It wasn't until I began entertaining that I realized just how calm and confident I had become in our tiny kitchen. Friends were amazed at the spreads I so effortlessly created for them. They marvelled at the stories of my extended family, and the dishes that complemented these, listening intently just as I had done in Mum's kitchen. I assured them if they spent the weekend with me in the kitchen, they would be equipped with enough insight to recreate the dishes at home for their family and friends. My girlfriends challenged me to this, insisting that I take their request seriously and find a space to share our stories and family recipes with them, an offer I initially declined.

However, I began expanding my recipe repertoire, listening to not only my mother and mother-in-law but other women in our community tell me about how they came to preserving their cultures and many of the memories attached to food. I sensed their nerves as they retold their stories of leaving home and settling in a new place; the familiar foods I had always grown up eating suddenly had a new sense of flavour and meaning. Many of these stories, although universal to most migrants regardless of their origins, often went untold in our community, out of fear, shame and often in a bid to forget. But they belonged in everybody's homes and reasserted one thing: the common thread we share as humans, our need for love, for connection, but ultimately to belong.

Through these stories I felt a connection to the Lebanese diaspora. I drew courage and a strong appreciation for my heritage, and preserving this became something I feel very strongly about.

After much persuading, Mum finally agreed to come along and help, as I gathered my friends and shared with them what would be the first of many 'Sunday Kitchen' cooking sessions. Initially daunted by the experience, we found the guests entranced by Mum's stories of my grandparents' flight from Lebanon, migrating and growing up in Australia and how food brought everyone together even in the most difficult of times. Each session I watched in awe as our guests related to the stories, giving context and deeper meaning to the dishes. Our recipes not only took flight in our cooking classes, our stories did too, and guests would share how they incorporated them into their own celebrations. Sourcing, planning and cooking a spread was no longer an unachievable dream but a reality full of soul. And ever since, our Sunday Kitchen has gone from strength to strength.

How to Best Use this Book

Learning to prepare a spread that works cohesively and feeds a group is a skill we believe everyone should have and is what we aim to share with you in this book.

We hope you use this book not only to bring your family and friends together around the table but also to bring people into the kitchen with you to help prepare for the spread you will share. The book should help you to understand what kind of cook you are and show you how to adjust flavours based on your preference and palate. And we are sure it will encourage you to go on a journey to source the freshest and most authentic ingredients you can get your hands on.

This book contains nine weekend spreads and chapters of traditional home-style desserts and drinks that tell the story of how Lebanese people gather at the weekend and how and what they cook for their families and friends.

Along the way I've written stories as to why certain dishes are included and their cultural context. The ingredients and the methods are written by Mum (Sivine).

The spreads are a guide to the dishes Mum would make and how they complement each other as part of a *sofra*, a spread that brings people together. The beauty of home cooking is that there are no strict rules, dishes are always interchangeable based on season and availability and, of course, customized to suit the guests. The recipes are also a guide, and a way to help you understand the ingredients that make up the dishes. Lebanese cooking relies on using all five senses, and we hope the spreads will give you the confidence to do so.

Some of these traditional Lebanese dishes require a little more time and preparation than a regular midweek meal so are traditionally reserved for the weekend, religious celebrations and special occasions. Start with three dishes per spread if you are feeling overwhelmed: the main, with a side of rice and salad usually works well.

Preparing elements and ingredients in advance is the secret to enjoyable cooking, no matter how small the task may be. To help you do the same, we have included a table with make-ahead notes at the end of each chapter to ensure the preparations for your weekend spread are easy and stress free. You don't need to strictly follow the preparation tables, but they give you a good idea of things you can do in advance.

Each spread is designed for a gathering and should feed ten people, but quantities can be easily adjusted to suit more or fewer people. Don't forget, it is customary for guests to take home some leftovers. If you are choosing dishes to make for a weekday meal, then you could halve the main recipes to feed four to six people and provide two side dishes, making about one-third of the quantities.

The wonderful thing about Lebanese food is that it is not rigid; many of the recipes within each spread can be interchanged depending on what you have access to, what you feel like and what is in season.

Essential Kitchen Tools

Most Lebanese kitchens would be likely to have every item on this list and you'll find that there is nothing out of the ordinary. Mum kept a tight and practical kitchen, and had nothing but a small food processor by way of appliances, opting to use her hands. Many of my most cherished kitchen heirlooms are tools that I have acquired from her.

Your Hands

'Your hands are your most valuable tools in the kitchen', I can hear Mum saying. She's right. Not only enhancing our connection to the ingredients, hands allow you to feel texture, temperature and consistency when cooking. Salads, stuffings and fillings should always be mixed by hand. I continue to marvel at the way Mum uses her hands to measure a *rasheh*, as she calls it, meaning a generous sprinkle, which measures about a tablespoon; another she did with her cupped hand, which was about three-quarters of a cup. Although at first it was frustrating to try to determine what a *rasheh* was, I now find myself using this same measuring system when cooking.

Equipment

Chopping board: Large wooden
Bowls: Wide stainless steel mixing bowls in assorted sizes to allow your hands and elbows in to mix freely
Colanders: Assorted sizes
Food processor
Hand pull chopper: This functions like a rough food processor but without electricity; it is compact, portable and perfect for chopping garlic, onions and herbs
Kitchen knife: Large sharp
Kitchen scales
Ladle
Lemon squeezer: The one that you place a halved lemon on top of and turn to extract the juice
***Maamoul* moulds:** For when baking *maamoul* (page 196)
Measuring spoons
Metal teapot and small glass cups: Lebanese *shai* must be served in these cups
Pestle and mortar: A large stone set, mainly for crushing garlic (always with salt)

Paring knives
Rakweh (Lebanese coffee pot) and small cups we call *shaffe*: Lebanese coffee is always served in these cups
Saucepans: Cast aluminium pots, non-stick
Sauté pans: Stainless steel, small and large
Serving spoons
Sieve
Spice grinder
Spoons: Wooden
Tongs
Whisk: Especially when mixing tahini to avoid clumping

Assortment of Serving Platters

When you go to all the trouble of making a large salad or layered rice dish, it's important to have appropriate bowls and platters to serve them on. I have a large range of serving dishes that I have collected over the last decade from vintage and second-hand stores, some new, mostly old, and all of them cherished.

Ovens

All ovens behave slightly differently, so you will need to keep that in mind and adjust times and temperatures to suit your particular oven. I have tested all the oven recipes in a fan oven at the temperatures given. If you are not cooking in a fan oven, you may need to increase the temperatures by a few degrees.

And finally...

Intention: Mum always cooked with love; it was evident in the way she meticulously sourced ingredients, the way she made time and space for cooking for her family and the way she brought people together through food – she argues you can always taste someone's intentions in their food.

The Lebanese Pantry

The scent of Mum's pantry has always been intoxicating – like opening an aromatic treasure chest, at all times stocked with the very best and most authentic ingredients she could source – dried herbs, spices, aromatics and nuts bought by the scoop. It was not particularly large, as she was always so mindful of waste and preferred to constantly replenish with fresh ingredients. It consisted of ingredients she made fresh at home, as well as those she sourced locally from grocers near and far, and the *mouneh* (artisan pantry staples) such as pomegranate molasses and rosewater she ordered from friends and family in Lebanon. I would accompany her on 'sourcing trips', as we called them, and together we travelled to different stores known for their quality ingredients.

There are so many ingredients found in the Lebanese pantry, each with endless possibilities and uses; however, this is a practical list and one I find captures everything you will need to make the meals in this book. Pantry ingredients should always live in a cool, dark place away from any heat and direct sunlight. You could even put things like nuts and spices in the fridge to extend their life.

Salt

According to my mother, salt is the most important ingredient when cooking. Understanding how to 'add salt to taste' is a skill that develops over time and, believe me, I still cringe when Mum takes the first mouthful of something I have cooked. Tasting your food while cooking is a crucial, and often overlooked, step and one that has transformed the way I understand flavour. We generally cook with finely ground sea salt, which is finer and dissolves well, though you can use what you are most comfortable with.

Spices and Aromatics

These are the traditional spices you will find commonly used in Lebanese cooking, followed by some recipes for spice blends. The homemade blends are those we use in the book but you can substitute ready-made blends if you prefer.

Aromatic mix

Mum's signature mix that she uses to infuse flavour in the stock for her lamb spread (page 74) is a combination of cinnamon, cloves, cardamom, bay leaves, star anise, dried lime and allspice berries. I keep a jar of these loose aromatics for when I am making the lamb spread. You can omit any of the aromatics based on your preference or use more or less of each ingredient if you wish.

Ground caraway

Caraway has fresh aniseed and fennel notes in its flavour profile as it is part of the same plant family.

Paprika

Sweet, mild or smoked, paprika is a great way to add an extra kick of flavour and colour to meat marinades, roasted vegetables or simply sprinkled on hummus.

Sumac

A sour, tangy, crushed deep purplish-red berry that we use generously in salads and stuffings or on vegetables, meat and fish.

Chilli

Chilli adds another dimension to Lebanese food. If you do not eat chilli, it can easily be omitted, but I strongly encourage you to use it as often as you like.

In the summer, we often buy a kilo of small, fresh red chillies and make our own dried chilli powder. If you have access to chillies and enough sunshine, I encourage you to do the same. Wear gloves when handling chillies and be careful not to touch your face, especially your mouth or eyes. Take any quantity of small red chillies and remove the green tops with your fingers. Place the chillies in a food processor and blitz them to a chunky, rough paste. Spread the paste on a stainless steel tray in the sun, turning and mixing occasionally, until the chillies have completely dried out. How long this takes will depend on where you are, the temperature and humidity, but will be about 2–3 weeks. Alternatively, spread them on baking trays in your oven at its lowest setting for about 6 hours. Place the dried chilli mixture in batches into a spice grinder or pestle and mortar and blitz to a fine powder. Store in an airtight glass jar for up to a year.

Aleppo chilli

Aleppo chilli, which originates in Hallab (Aleppo), Syria, offers a low to moderate heat with a somewhat smoky, fruity flavour. The texture is also much coarser than ground chilli.

Ground cinnamon

Cinnamon is used in both savoury and sweet Lebanese dishes and brings so much warmth and nostalgia to the kitchen.

Cumin

Both ground cumin and seeds are commonly used in Lebanese cooking. Of the two varieties, the greenish ones are most popular as they are more aromatic.

Dried herbs

We use a variety of dried herbs in salads, dips and spice mixes or to flavour vegetables, meats and fish. Mint, parsley, oregano, basil, marjoram and coriander (cilantro) are the most commonly used. Once you begin drying your own herbs, you will immediately notice their potent aroma and vibrant flavour.

Mum has a table in the sunniest spot on the front porch of the house dedicated to drying her fresh herbs. Whenever she has a surplus, she picks them off their stems and lays them on stainless steel trays in the sun to dry out. Once dry, they should be crispy and crush easily and be stored in a container in the pantry. If they feel more leathery than crisp, place them on a tray in the oven at its lowest setting or in the microwave between two pieces of paper towel for 30 seconds or so.

Sabaa Bharat
Seven-spice Bharat

This is the signature scent of Lebanese cooking, a classic spice blend consisting of seven spices. Ratios often vary from each region and generally each family will have their own recipe.

Makes about 150g (5oz)
2 tbsp black peppercorns
3 tbsp cumin seeds
3 tsp coriander seeds
3 tsp grated nutmeg
1 tsp cloves
1 cinnamon stick
3 tsp allspice (pimento) berries

If using whole spices, grind them in a spice grinder or with a pestle and mortar to create a smooth powder. You may have to sift out any chunky pieces through a fine sieve. If using ground spices, place them in a bowl and combine well. Stored in an airtight glass jar, they will last for several months.

Kammouneh
Cumin and Herb Spice Mix

Kammouneh is a spice mix from the south of Lebanon, synonymous with making the ground beef dishes Frakeh and Kibbeh (pages 72 and 179), and each village and family has their own variation. Mum used to tell me about the southern Lebanese women selling freshly mixed *kammouneh*, dried rose petals, marjoram, basil and spices piled on trays in front of their houses.

Kammoun (cumin) is the primary ingredient in this fragrant mix, which can be used as a rub on meat or roasted vegetables. We use most of the aromatics whole but combining ground spices will work well, too. Pictured opposite.

Makes about 200g (7oz)
15g (½oz) dried mint
15g (½oz) dried marjoram
15g (½oz) dried basil
2 tbsp cumin seeds
1 tbsp allspice (pimento) berries
1 tbsp Sabaa Bharat (left)
3 tbsp ground cumin
½ tbsp ground cloves
2 tbsp dried rose petals
½ cinnamon stick, broken up
½ tbsp ground cinnamon
½ tbsp ground black pepper

Place all the ingredients in a mixing bowl and mix well. Stored in an airtight glass jar, the mix will last for several months.

Za'atar Baladi
Traditional Za'atar

Za'atar is the Arabic name for the green wild thyme that is dried and used to create the spice blend of the same name. Many native varieties of za'atar grow in the Levant, with its thin, spiky green leaves and purple flowers, which produce quite a spicy, hearty, earthy flavour – with variations throughout the region. The za'atar spice blend consists of dried thyme, sumac, toasted sesame seeds and salt.

Makes about 150g (5oz)
20g (¾oz/⅔ cup) native Lebanese za'atar or 15g (½oz/⅓ cup) dried thyme and 15g (½oz/⅓ cup) dried oregano
15g (½oz/⅓ cup) sumac
40g (1½oz/¼ cup) toasted sesame seeds
sea salt, to taste

Place the dried herbs, sumac and sesame seeds in a dry frying pan (skillet) on a low heat and combine until fragrant, then season with salt and leave to cool. Store in an airtight glass jar for up to 6 months.

Za'atar Halabi
Za'atar from Aleppo

This za'atar blend comes from the city of Hallab (Aleppo) in Syria. Mum's many Syrian friends would often gift us jars of *za'atar halabi* and, if I am honest, I prefer it for its melody of spices and nutty texture.

Makes about 200g (3½oz)
2 tbsp dried aniseed
2 tsp fennel seeds
3 tsp cumin seeds
2 tsp ground coriander
1 tbsp sumac
50g (2oz/⅓ cup) toasted sesame seeds
60g (2oz/2 cups) Za'atar Baladi (page 20)

Grind the aniseed, fennel and cumin seeds in a spice grinder until fluffy, sift out any impurities and place in a mixing bowl. Add the coriander, sumac and sesame seeds along with the za'atar and combine well. Store in an airtight glass jar for up to 6 months.

Legumes and Grains

Fine brown bulgur wheat
Bulgur wheat (burghul) is made from whole grain wheat that has been boiled, dried and ground. It has a subtle, nutty flavour and is found in dishes all over the Levant, as well as Egypt and Turkey. To this day, it is still made by hand in Lebanese villages as part of their *mouneh* supply and comes in a variety of sizes from coarse to very fine. Fine bulgur wheat does not need to be cooked, as once it absorbs any moisture from other ingredients, it expands and can be eaten straight away.

Chickpeas
Growing up, we only ever had dried chickpeas (garbanzos) in the pantry and cooked chickpeas in the freezer, so there was never a need for the canned variety, although they are handy if you are short of time. About 350g (12oz/2 cups) of dried chickpeas is equivalent to 1kg (2lb 4oz/6½ cups) of cooked chickpeas, plenty to make a share plate of hummus.

To prepare dried chickpeas, soak them overnight in plenty of water. The next day, drain the chickpeas and rinse them well. Put in a large saucepan with 1 teaspoon of bicarbonate of soda (baking soda), cover with fresh water and bring to the boil. Remove any foam on the surface and reduce the heat to low. Cover the chickpeas and cook for about an hour until just tender. The skins should remain intact and the chickpeas whole. Use immediately or, to store in the freezer, leave the pan to cool to room temperature before placing the chickpeas in sealed bags or containers, along with their cooking water.

Fava beans

In the UK, fava beans are usually known as broad beans and are cooked fresh from the pods. In Lebanon we use the dried beans from the smaller-bean varieties of the same plant.

They are traditionally eaten for breakfast, and the dried bags can be handy when you are serving a large group. However, cans work very well, too, especially when combined with freshly boiled chickpeas. You can also buy cans containing a mixture of both.

Ensure the dried fava beans are a rich golden brown colour; avoid the very dark ones that may have been on the shelf for some time.

To prepare dried fava beans, soak them overnight in plenty of water. The next day, drain the beans and rinse them well. Put in a large saucepan with plenty of water and 1 teaspoon of bicarbonate of soda (baking soda) and bring to the boil, then reduce the heat to low and cook for 3–4 hours, stirring frequently to avoid lumps and to stop any sticking to the bottom of the pan. After 3½ hours, test to see if they are cooked; when ready, they will easily pop out of their skins.

Green lentils

Green lentils are used in many vegetarian dishes. They can be bought dried. Simply boil for about 20 minutes until tender.

Moghrabieh

Moghrabieh translates to 'from Maghreb', or Morocco, and refers to hand-rolled balls of cracked wheat, flour and water that were brought to Palestine, where they are also called *maftoul*. They are essentially large pearl couscous rolled by hand.

Medium-grain rice

Medium-grain white rice is the main rice used in traditional Lebanese cooking and has a moist, tender and slightly chewy texture that makes it perfect for stuffing. Always wash the rice to remove the starch by rinsing it in a bowl under cold water until the water runs clear. This should be done just before you are about to cook and never earlier.

Long-grain Sella rice

This is not to be confused with traditional basmati rice, which is fluffier. Sella rice is partially pre-cooked in its inedible husk before being processed for eating. Parboiling is a step before milling the rice, which helps transfer and preserve the nutrients of the bran. While not traditional to Lebanese cooking, Mum uses this rice particularly when entertaining and cooking larger quantities, as although it takes slightly longer to cook, it is very forgiving and always cooks evenly with the grains remaining separate. Always wash before use (see above).

Semolina

Semolina is a flour made from durum wheat, which comes either fine or coarsely ground and is used in a variety of Lebanese sweets. Fine semolina is often used in place of flour as it has a delicious crumbly texture, whereas coarse semolina can be used in anything from cakes to breads.

Nuts and Seeds

Nuts and seeds are significant in the Lebanese pantry and feature everywhere from savoury to sweet dishes. Nuts are especially used in feasting spreads to adorn rice dishes. Sourcing the best-quality nuts you can find is often crucial to the overall dish, particularly when they are crushed and stuffed into desserts.

Frequently used nuts include halved blanched almonds, cashews, pistachios and walnuts.

Nigella seeds

Nigella seeds have a strong, nutty aroma and when used in savoury dishes have hints of onion, oregano and black pepper. They pair remarkably well with cheeses.

Pine nuts

Lebanese pine nuts are renowned as some of the best in the world, known for their long, slender shape and delicious nutty flavour. They are hard to acquire and can be quite expensive, so other pine nut varieties are a good substitute, and flaked (slivered) almonds work fine, too.

Sesame seeds

White sesame seeds are most commonly used and are always kept raw before being toasted to add to Za'atar (page 20).

Other Ingredients

Lebanese bread

Lebanese bread is served at every meal, pillowy and soft when sourced fresh every few days from the local bakery or supermarket. Its shelf life is extended if kept in the fridge for up to a week and it freezes very well.

Ghee

Also known as clarified butter, ghee is a delicacy used sparingly in Lebanese cuisine to add a delicate nutty, buttery flavour. It is also commonly used in place of butter in most desserts.

Mahlab

Mahlab grains are small and pear-shaped with a light brown husk and soft core and come from the seeds of the black cherry. They are sold whole or ground and have a subtle aromatic flavour, mainly used in biscuits such as Bascot bil Tamer (page 204). If you cannot find *mahlab*, leave it out of the recipe.

Mastic

Pronounced 'miskeh' in Arabic, mastic is the resin collected from a tree (*Pistacias lentiscus*) native to Greece and Turkey. It is ground finely and used in small amounts to flavour puddings such as Wahel al Jannah (page 211) or ice creams, adding a mild, sweet flavour that is traditional to the Mediterranean.

Extra virgin olive oil

A good-quality extra virgin olive oil will transform the way you prepare and eat Lebanese food. Many Lebanese families import the oil from their villages in a bid to support and keep the production alive. We primarily use it for dressing all salads, cheese and dips or eat it fresh with bread and raw meats.

Neutral oil for frying
This refers to any oil you prefer to use for frying: rapeseed (canola), vegetable, sunflower, light olive oil. It should have a high smoke point and no bitter after-taste. We often leave it to cool and fill glass jars with the strained oil to re-use two or three times.

Pomegranate molasses
This syrup is made by boiling sour pomegranate seeds until they are reduced to a thick, dark brown liquid and is used to add a subtle sweet and sour flavour to dishes. It is famously used in the dressing for Fattoush (page 83) and adds a strong kick when combined with lemon juice, garlic and olive oil to marinate or drizzle. Source it from authentic grocers, where the product is usually less sweet.

Rosewater and orange blossom water
These fragrant waters are prominent ingredients in Lebanese sweets and are made by distilling the petals of a native rose, or the blossom flowers of Seville oranges. They are often combined in the same recipe to create the signature taste and aroma of Lebanese desserts.

Tahini
When cooking Lebanese food, sourcing an authentic Middle Eastern tahini is crucial. The varieties vary considerably in taste and texture; look for a very light colour and a runny texture. Keep in mind that tahini separates from cream to oil and requires thorough mixing before each use.

Tomato purée (paste)
When in-season tomatoes are harvested in the Lebanese villages; they are turned into an authentic, deep-red, caramelized tomato paste with a punchy flavour.

Pickles and Preserved Ingredients
Pickled and preserved vegetables are an essential part of the Lebanese table and are always presented on a platter, adding punchy and spicy flavours to any spread, or serving as a palate cleanser.

It is very common for families to continue this historical method of preserving vegetables at home as part of the season's *mouneh* (pantry staples), although if you are short of time there are great varieties available In Middle Eastern stores. Pickling at home is very simple, and watching the vegetables in the glass jars change colour in the weeks and months only adds to the anticipation of opening the jar to taste.

Try to use a very good-quality vinegar and olive oil. Sterilize the water by boiling it first and allowing it to cool completely; this step is crucial. Also make sure you wash and sterilize the jars, which can be done by washing them well and placing them in a 140°C/275°F (gas 3) oven on a baking tray for up to half an hour before turning the oven off and leaving the jars to cool.

Mkhalal
Pickling Solution

The most common solution for pickling consists of vinegar and water at a 1:2 ratio. Rock salt is the only salt that should be used. This is enough pickling solution for a 1-litre (34fl oz/4-cup) jar filled with about 1kg (2lb 4oz) of vegetables, depending on the type and their weight.

Makes about 600ml (20fl oz/2½ cups)
400ml (13fl oz/generous 1½ cups) water
200ml (7fl oz/scant 1 cup) distilled
  white vinegar
3 tbsp rock salt

Mix the water, vinegar and salt in a jug until the salt is completely diluted. Add the brine to your chosen vegetables, adjusting the quantities accordingly.

Kabees Leffet
Pickled Turnips

These turnips pickled with beetroot are the bright pink pickles we Lebanese are famous for.

Makes a 1-litre (34fl oz/4-cup) jar
1kg (2lb 4oz) white turnips
1 small beetroot (beet)
a handful of rock salt
1 quantity of Mkhalal (above)

Remove the leaves from the vegetables and give them a good wash with a scrubbing brush. Chop the turnips into 1cm (¾in) thick discs and then into large matchsticks. Cut the beetroot in eighths and set aside. Put the turnips in a mixing bowl, combine with the rock salt and leave to rest for 2 hours.

Strain the water from the turnips and wash the vegetables. Layer the turnips and beetroot in a sterilized jar, then fill with the pickling solution. Close the jar and store in a cool dark place. Eat after 3–4 weeks.

Kabees Arnabeet
Pickled Cauliflower

I love the addition of the garlic and chilli with these pickled vegetables, which are great to snack on with mezza.

Makes a 1-litre (34fl oz/4-cup) jar
500g (1lb 2oz) cauliflower
6 baby (Dutch) carrots (optional)
2 small red chillies (optional)
2 whole garlic cloves, peeled (optional)
1 quantity of Mkhalal (above left)

Cut the cauliflower into medium-sized florets, wash them well along with the carrots, removing the green tops and ensuring there are no strands on the ends. Blanch the carrots and cauliflower in boiling water for 3 seconds to kill any bacteria, then place in cold water to stop them from cooking further.

Wash the chillies well and remove the tops. Pack the cauliflower, carrots, chilli and garlic into a sterilized jar. Pour in the pickling solution to cover the vegetables and close the jar. Place a small tray or plate underneath the jar, as it will likely overflow in the first week, then set aside in a cool, dark place. Eat after 2 weeks and within 3–6 months. Store in the fridge after opening.

Zaytoun
Table Olives

I encourage everyone not to be daunted
by the idea of preserving their own olives
– they are ready to eat within a month of
making them and can last up to 12 months
in the fridge.

Makes a 2-litre (70fl oz/8-cup) jar
2kg (4lb 8oz) small green olives
2 lemons with leaves
6 small red chillies (more if desired)
5 wild fennel stems with fronds
about 200g (7oz) rock salt
2 litres (70fl oz/8 cups) water
2 tbsp coriander seeds
a handful of wild thyme (optional)
about 250ml (8½fl oz/1 cup) olive oil

Using a pestle, gently crack the olives until
they have just split. Do this in one swift
motion to avoid bruising, then place in a
bowl of cold water and set aside for 1 hour.

Meanwhile, wash all the fresh ingredients
and dry them well. Slice the lemons and
cut each slice into quarters. Remove the
tips of the chillies and cut up the fennel
stems and fronds into 8cm (3¼in) lengths.

For the brine, mix the salt and the water
in the ratio of 100g (3½oz) of salt per
1 litre (34fl oz/4 cups) of water. To test the
saltiness, place an egg in the salted water.
If it floats, it is the right ratio.

Drain the olives, then add the lemons,
leaves, fennel, chillies, seeds and thyme
along with half of the oil and combine
with your hands, setting aside a few lemon
leaves to cover the top of the olives.

Begin to fill a sterilized glass jar with the
olives, with the other ingredients evenly
distributed throughout. Fill the jar with
the brine and add the oil to the top, then
finally cover the olives with the reserved
lemon leaves and an extra tablespoon of
salt, before sealing the jar. Store in a cool,
dark place.

Kabees Harr
Pickled Chillies

These pickled chillies are definitely
something you should consider making,
especially to eat with Salatet foul
Medammas (page 58) for breakfast or
alongside a big barbecue.

Makes a 1-litre (34fl oz/4-cup) jar
500g (1lb 2oz) small green chillies
1 quantity of Mkhalal (page 26)

Wash the chillies well, drain, then place
them in a sterilized jar standing up. It is
easiest to do this if you place the jar on
its side. Stand it upright and pour in the
pickling solution. Close the jar and store in
a cool dark place. Eat after 3–4 weeks.

Kabees Khyar
Pickled Cucumbers

Every Lebanese person has several jars
of these at home, to be eaten alongside
every meal.

Makes a 1-litre (34fl oz/4-cup) jar
500g (1lb 2oz) small Lebanese cucumbers
1 quantity of Mkhalal (page 26)

Wash the cucumbers well, removing
any small leaves at the tip. Using the
tip of a sharp knife, make several small
cuts all around the cucumber. Stand the
cucumbers upright in the sterilized jar and
pack them in tightly. Pour in the pickling
solution to cover, then close the jar and
store in a cool, dark place. Eat after
2–3 weeks.

Makdous
Preserved Stuffed Aubergines

You can find these spicy aubergines alongside the pickles in Middle Eastern stores, but this homemade version is incomparable. My mother-in-law's friend Samar gave me this recipe after I tried hers and fell in love with them.

Makes a 1-litre (34fl oz/4-cup) jar
1kg (2lb 4oz) tiny purple or striped
    aubergines (eggplants) about the
    size of a golf ball
2 romano peppers
150g (5oz/1½ cups) walnuts
4 garlic cloves, minced
4 red chillies, deseeded and finely chopped
    (optional)
olive oil, as needed
rock salt, as needed

Wash the aubergines and place them in a saucepan of boiling water, with a plate on top to stop them floating to the surface, and boil for 15 minutes. Drain, then place in a bowl of cold water to stop them from cooking further. Once cool, remove and leave to rest for 15 minutes in a colander.

Set up a bowl with a perforated tray on top and lay a dish towel on top of the tray; set aside. Take a sharp paring knife and remove the tops of the aubergines as close to the tip as possible, then slice through half of the aubergine to open it up without cutting through to the other side. Place a small pinch of rock salt inside the flesh of each aubergine and place on the dish towel with the opening facing down. Lay another dish towel on top and a plate or tray large enough to cover all the aubergines. Place a heavy weight on top of that to extract moisture from the aubergines, which will improve the quality of your *makdous*. Leave to strain for 24 hours in a cool place.

Meanwhile, slice the peppers and remove all seeds. Place them in a food processor and blitz until minced, then strain them overnight in a fine sieve to remove all the moisture.

To make the stuffing, chop the walnuts with a knife and place in a mixing bowl with the garlic and chilli. Add the red pepper paste and combine well. Remove the weight from the aubergines and discard any liquid that has been strained. Wearing gloves, open up an aubergine and stuff about 1 heaped teaspoon of the stuffing mixture into the cavity. Place the aubergines on a plate, and repeat until they are all filled. Wipe each one with paper towel to clean, then fit them tightly into a sterilized jar. Top up with olive oil and close. Place in a cool, dark place and open after 4 weeks.

Pomegranates
Remman

Pomegranates are a key ingredient in many Lebanese recipes. Here I've included a simple method to make the most of your pomegranate seeds.

1 pomegranate

Begin by slicing small cuts around the flower of the pomegranate, only going as far as the skin, creating a pentagon shape. Using a sharp paring knife, lift the skin and you should see a core that runs through the centre of the fruit. Slice around the pomegranate, remembering to only go as far as the skin, and gently pull apart the pieces from one another. Remove the core and gently begin to push off the small seeds from the inner skin. Most of the seeds should be undamaged and store well in an airtight container in a fridge for up to a week.

Shanklish
Spicy Fermented Yogurt

Shanklish is a fermented curd cheese seasoned with salt and chilli and shaped into balls the size of small oranges.

The process is wonderfully simple; it just requires time for the cheese to dry. To have it on hand for weekend breakfasts, we usually make a batch large enough to freeze. Use good-quality yogurt.

Makes 5 x 200g (7oz) balls
3kg (6lb 8oz) pot of set yogurt
2–3 tbsp sea salt
1 tbsp chilli powder (or to taste)
extra virgin olive oil
Za'atar Baladi (page 20)

Empty the yogurt into a large saucepan and add a heaped tablespoon of salt and 500ml (17fl oz/2 cups) of water, stir, then place over a very low heat to warm up until you could dip your finger in the liquid and it would be hot but not burn.

Allow the yogurt to simmer, making sure you don't stir it, and eventually the curd and whey will separate. This should take about 1–2 hours.

Leave it to cool and then tip the contents of the pan into a colander lined with several layers of muslin (cheesecloth), secure it closed and place into a colander overnight in the fridge to continue to drain.

Lay 3–4 dish towels on a tray, place the cheese in the muslin onto the towels and spread out evenly to dry, uncovered, for about 4–6 days, putting it back into the fridge overnight. You may need to change the dish towels a few times, as they will be soaked with water.

Once the *shanklish* is soft and dry, remove from the tray and place in a large mixing bowl. Add a tablespoon of salt and the chilli powder and combine with your hands. Collect a handful of cheese and compress with your hands to make a ball shape, about the size of a tennis ball, making sure it is tight, compact and sturdy.

Place the balls on a tray covered with 2–3 dish towels to strain further and put in the fridge or on the work surface for 2 days. Place some extra virgin olive oil in a bowl and some za'atar in a separate bowl. Dip each ball in the oil to coat, then roll it around in the dried za'atar.

You can keep them stored in the fridge for up to 3 months, or in the freezer for up to 6 months.

Terwikat
Al' Dayaa

A Village
Breakfast

Breadmaking in the villages of Lebanon is a sacred, traditional practice passed down through generations of families. For many, the process is a communal activity amongst family, friends and neighbours who come together to share the workload and exchange tips, techniques and a little village gossip.

The breadmaking typically starts at dawn with the preparation of the dough, made from a whole wheat flour, water, yeast and salt. The dough is kneaded by hand or machine, depending on the quantity, and left to rise for several hours before the baking begins.

Historically there are two methods used for breadmaking: the *tannour*, a large round clay pot heated by burning wood or charcoal inside, or the *saj*, a dome-shaped oven with a large, flat surface used for baking *khobz marqouk* (thin mountain bread), often topped with za'atar and various cheeses.

With Mum being from the city, we did not grow up making breakfast pastries at home, and living in an area densely populated with the Lebanese community, we didn't have to. An abundance of Lebanese bakeries, with large ovens and *saj* domes, meant the pastries were accessible and cheap. Mum would prepare the fillings and we would take them to the bakery where they would fill and bake fresh pastries, something my grandmother also did in Tripoli long ago.

It is now in the chaos of life that I truly cherish these slow weekend breakfasts spent pottering around the kitchen assembling this spread, the practice both meditative and restorative. My daughters look forward to it the most, rolling out the dough balls ready for me to fill them and sitting eagerly by the oven door waiting for the first batch to come out.

By all means, start with only the pastries and perhaps the *labne* and a plate of fresh vegetables, as we often do, and work your way to the rest. Olives, *labne* and *shanklish* can be made well in advance or bought from Middle Eastern grocers if you are short of time. Don't forget the *shai* and *ahweh* (tea and coffee)!

Ajin
The Dough

This dough is simple, versatile and incredibly forgiving. I prepare this with my hands – the aim is to keep it as hydrated and sticky as possible, while ensuring it is still easy to handle. The whole wheat and oil make this dough light and thin, giving the pastries a crunchy exterior when baked. Best of all, this dough can be made up to 3 days ahead and freezes well. The recipe accounts for the fact that you will want to make at least a dozen of each of the pastries on the following pages; however, you can halve this recipe and it works out just fine.

1kg (2lb 4oz/8 cups) self-raising (self-rising) flour, plus extra for dusting
1kg (2lb 4oz/8 cups) whole wheat flour
7g (1 sachet) instant yeast
1 heaped tbsp sea salt
1 heaped tbsp caster (superfine) sugar
1.2 litres (43fl oz/5 cups) lukewarm water
250ml (8½floz/1 cup) olive oil
300g (10½oz/2 cups) pre-soaked
   yellow cornmeal

Sift the flours into a large bowl and add the yeast, salt and sugar. Combine with a hand whisk and make a well in the centre.

In a mixing jug, add 1 litre (34fl oz/4 cups) of the lukewarm water with the oil and stir to combine. Gradually add the water mixture to the dough, using a wooden spoon to combine gently, ensuring most has come together into a shaggy mixture. If you need to, add the remaining water to ensure no flour is left in the bowl. Ideally the mixture should be moist yet manageable; don't be afraid to add more water or flour, if required.

Scrape the sticky dough onto a floured work surface and knead for 5 minutes. Continue to knead and incorporate the dough until all the water and flour have been combined.

To prove the dough, you must first make smaller balls that will be rolled out to make the pastries. Wet a few J-cloths (Chux) and use them to cover the base of the tray or container you intend to let the balls of dough prove in, keeping one wet cloth to lay on top.

For the Fatayer (page 40) and the Lahem bi Ajin (page 44) I like to use 40g (1½oz) of dough and for the Za'atar Manoushe (page 44), 75g (3oz). I keep a scale handy for checking. Before you begin rolling out the smaller balls, put the cornmeal in a small bowl and keep it handy. Roll each ball of dough around in the palm of your hand or on the table, neatly tucking it under itself. Once you have rolled the dough into balls, roll the balls in the fine cornmeal, place on the prepared tray and cover with the wet cloth. It is important the dough feels moist so the cornmeal will stick to it, as it protects the dough from sticking together when proving, as well as giving the baked pastries a crispy texture.

Place the covered tray in a warm place to rest for 2 hours.

After 2 hours, the dough is ready to use. Alternatively, you can store it in an airtight container in the fridge – lined with wet J-cloths – for up to 3 days and in the freezer for up to 3 months.

Fatayer
Spinach Turnovers

What I love most about these pastries is how the seasons determine the filling. These freeze well, too.

½ quantity of Ajin (page 38), plus flour
  for dusting
4 bunches of English spinach
2 large onions, finely diced
2 medium-sized tomatoes, finely diced
1 tbsp sumac
1 tsp Sabaa Bharat (page 20)
1 tsp chilli powder (optional)
juice of 1 lemon
2 tbsp pomegranate molasses
2 tbsp olive oil
1 tsp citric acid (optional, but this helps to
  enhance the lemon flavour)
sea salt, to taste
1 lemon, cut into wedges, to serve

Prepare the Ajin dough (see page 38) and leave it to rest while you begin to make the filling.

Spinach carries plenty of moisture and it is crucial this is drawn out before filling the pastries. Begin by washing the spinach and finely chopping it. Place it in a mixing bowl with a heaped tablespoon of salt, mix and set aside for 5 minutes. The salt will begin to wilt the spinach and help to draw out the moisture.

Begin squeezing large handfuls of the spinach into the sink or a separate bowl, ensuring you squeeze out as much liquid as possible. Place the wilted spinach in a large, clean mixing bowl.

Add the onions and tomatoes to the bowl with the remaining ingredients. Using clean hands, combine the mixture well, tasting it to adjust the seasoning to your liking, and set aside to allow the flavours to develop while the dough is resting. It is important to note the flavours of the spinach filling should be overpoweringly sour and lemony while uncooked to allow for any flavour that lessens during cooking.

Preheat your oven to 200°C/400°F (gas 8) and lightly oil a baking tray.

Dust your work surface with flour and, once the dough has rested, roll out each ball into a circle, using a rolling pin, and place 1 heaped tablespoon of the filling in the middle. Fold over two sides of the circle to the centre to make a triangle point and pinch down, then bring up the bottom of the triangle, pinching it along the middle (pictured opposite). Repeat until you have used up your filling.

Once your triangles are ready, line up the pastries on the prepared baking tray. Bake for about 15 minutes, or until they are golden brown on the top and bottom.

Serve with extra lemon wedges.

Below preparing *fatayer*

Lebanese bakeries traditionally use a mixture of spinach, onion, sumac and lemon, but you are free to use whatever you like. I like to use home-grown *bakleh* (purslane) in summer for its tangy and earthy flavour.

Breakfast pastries are the hero of this spread, encircled by complementary dishes.

Za'atar Manoushe
Flatbread with Za'atar

These flatbreads are not meant to be perfect, so relax, roll up your sleeves, clear your mind and enjoy the process.

½ quantity of Ajin (page 38)
100g (3½oz) Za'atar Baladi (page 20) or Za'atar Halabi (page 22)
250ml (8½fl oz/1 cup) olive oil, plus extra as needed

Prepare the Ajin dough (see page 38) and leave it to rest at room temperature while you begin to make the filling.

Mix together the za'atar and oil.

Place a 25cm (10in) cast iron pan or non-stick frying pan (skillet) on the stove over a high heat. Once hot, turn the heat down to medium. On a clean, flat surface, smear some olive oil, place your ball of room-temperature dough in the middle and begin to push it out as if you were making a pizza. When the circle is about the size of a fist, spread a tablespoon of the za'atar and oil mixture over the dough, using your fingertips to press the dough into shape. Spread it out quite thinly, and do not worry about it sticking, as you have oil underneath. It does not matter if you create small holes.

Once the pan is hot, lift the thin piece of dough and place it on the pan, leave it to sizzle and cook on the base for a few minutes. The dough should start making little air pockets. Leave it to go very crispy on the base before removing it.

You do not need to cook the side with the za'atar, as this technique is imitating the saj dome (page 37) and the manoushe cooks from the bottom up.

Serve with labne, olives and a platter of fresh vegetables.

Lahem bi Ajin
Meat Pastries

Try these hot out of the oven, with a spoonful of labne or Greek yogurt, a sprinkle of Aleppo chilli and a generous squeeze of lemon – truly the perfect savoury snack.

½ quantity of Ajin (page 38), plus flour for dusting
4 medium-sized tomatoes, finely diced
2 medium-sized onions, finely diced
500g (1lb 4oz) coarsely minced (ground) lamb or beef or both
1 tsp Sabaa Bharat (page 20)
1 tsp paprika
1 heaped tbsp tomato purée (paste)
2 tbsp pomegranate molasses
sea salt, to taste

Prepare the Ajin dough (see page 38) and leave it to rest while you begin to make the filling.

Put the tomatoes and onions in a large mixing bowl. Add the minced meat, spices, tomato purée, pomegranate molasses and salt. Using your hands, combine and knead the ingredients until all the meat is flavoured and all the ingredients are incorporated.

Preheat your oven to 200°C/400°F (gas 6) and lightly oil a baking tray or line with baking parchment.

Dust your work surface with flour and, once the dough has rested, roll out each ball, using either a rolling pin or your fingers, into a circle. Fill the centre with the mince filling and spread around the dough, keeping it away from the edges. Pinch the dough at the corners to enclose the mixture, leaving the middle exposed (as pictured on page 43). Repeat with the remaining dough and filling.

Put the pastries on the prepared tray. Bake for about 15 minutes, or until they are golden.

Below *za'atar manoushe* and
lahem bi ajin

Each region in Lebanon has a version of *lahem bi ajin* (meat pastries), from Tripoli to Baalbek to the south, and each family has an adopted recipe and method unique to them.

Labne
Strained Yogurt

Labne belongs on every breakfast
table and is perfect spread on a
Za'atar Manoushe (page 44) with fresh
mint, olives, tomatoes and cucumber.
Homemade *labne* topped with olive oil
lasts in the fridge for a few weeks so
it is worth making it yourself. Leave it to
strain for slightly longer, for a thicker,
creamier texture.

1 tbsp sea salt
2kg (4lb 8oz) plain yogurt
olive oil, as needed

Start by adding the salt to the yogurt,
mix well and taste, adjusting if desired.
Place the yogurt in a muslin (cheesecloth)
and then in a colander above a bowl in
the fridge. Leave the yogurt to strain
for at least 12 hours, depending on how
thick you like it. The longer you leave the
yogurt to strain, the thicker the *labne*
becomes. Once you are satisfied with the
consistency, taste for salt and either serve
as a dip garnished with extra virgin olive
oil or empty the *labne* into a container,
top with olive oil and place in the fridge
for up to 2 weeks.

Salatet Shanklish
Fermented Cheese Salad

Traditionally, *shanklish* is a village cheese,
made at home; however, you can find it
in the fridges of many Middle Eastern
grocers. It is rich and creamy due to the
straining of the yogurt and has a spicy
and salty flavour. For breakfast it is
prepared as a salad; the spice from the
chilli and freshness of the vegetables
make for a heavenly match with
the pastries.

1–2 balls of Shanklish (page 33)
300g (10½oz) cherry tomatoes, quartered
a handful of oregano leaves, picked
1 small red onion, finely chopped
1 long chilli, finely sliced
sea salt
a drizzle of extra virgin olive oil
zest of ½ lemon

In a small bowl, gently break up the
shanklish, allowing for some pieces to
be chunkier than others, then add the
tomatoes, oregano, onion and chilli.
Season with salt and drizzle with olive oil
before finally garnishing with lemon zest.
Serve cold.

Bayd a Soujouk
Fluffy Fried Eggs Topped with
a Spicy Fragrant Sausage

The Armenian community in Lebanon is
one of the largest and oldest in the world.
Many Armenian ingredients have become
staples of Lebanese cuisine, including
soujouk, a fragrant, spicy sausage found
in most Middle Eastern grocers and
butchers. It is sliced very thinly and served
either on top of fried eggs or on a plate
as a side dish. Once cooked, the sausage
releases a dark red, fragrant oil from the
red pepper paste in the filling, which you
can use to either fry your eggs or drizzle
all over once cooked.

250g (9oz) spicy soujouk
1 tbsp ghee
6 free-range eggs
sea salt, to taste
a pinch of freshly ground black pepper
120ml (4fl oz/½ cup) milk
a pinch of Aleppo chilli, to garnish

Begin by removing the thin casing around
the soujouk, and slicing it 2mm thick with
a sharp knife. Heat a wide frying pan
(skillet) and add the ghee. Once hot,
add the soujouk slices and move them
around the pan to fry evenly on each side
for a few minutes; it is important not to
overcook it as it will become chewy.

Remove the soujouk and place in a bowl,
reserving the oil in the pan. Crack the
eggs into a small mixing bowl, season well
with salt and pepper, add the milk and
whisk well. While the oil is hot, add the egg
mixture to the pan and cook as you would
scrambled eggs, or to your liking. Turn
off the heat and add the fried soujouk to
the top of the eggs, then garnish with the
Aleppo chilli and serve immediately.

Bayd a Toum
Eggs and Garlic Chives

Serve these simple eggs straight from
the pan with fresh Lebanese bread and
homemade olives, as my oldest friend
Terri's tayta (grandmother) would.

2 bunches of fresh garlic chives
6 free-range eggs
sea salt, to taste
2 tbsp olive oil
a pinch of Aleppo chilli, to garnish
fresh Lebanese bread, to serve
lemon wedges, to serve

Wash the chives well and pat them dry
before chopping them into 5mm (¼in)
lengths. Crack the eggs into a bowl and
season with salt, whisking them well until
fluffy. Add the olive oil to a frying pan
(skillet) over a medium heat. Reserve a
handful of the chives for garnish, then add
the rest to the pan, turning occasionally
until fragrant. Add the eggs to the pan
and let them cook gently on one side
before moving slightly to cook the other
side, like making scrambled egg. Garnish
with the reserved chives and a pinch of
ground Aleppo chilli. Serve immediately
with fresh Lebanese bread and wedges
of lemon.

The day before
* Make the dough and leave to prove
* Wash all the greens for the *fatayer* and leave to
  dry naturally
* Wash the vegetables and fresh herbs and leave to dry
  before storing in an airtight bag in the fridge
* Finely chop any tomatoes and onions to use for
  both *fatayer* and *lahem bi ajin*, placing them in
  separate containers
* Strain the yogurt to make the *labne*
* Once the dough has proved, place it in an airtight container
  in the fridge
* If the *shanklish* is frozen, put it in the fridge to
  defrost overnight
* Finely slice the *soujouk* and set aside, covered, in the fridge
* Roughly chop the chives and set aside, covered, in
  the fridge

On the day
* Take out the dough from the fridge and bring to
  room temperature
* Make the *fatayer* filling and set aside
* Make the *lahem bi ajin* filling and set aside
* Combine the za'atar with the oil and set aside
* Roll out the dough and begin filling the pastries
* Bake the *lahem bi ajin* and *fatayer*

While the pastries are baking
* Finely chop the ingredients for the *shanklish* salad
* Assemble the vegetable platter
* Place the olives in a serving bowl
* Place the *labne* in a serving dish and drizzle with extra
  virgin olive oil
* Roll out the flatbread with your fingers and make the
  za'atar *manoush* on the stove
* Assemble the *shanklish* salad and serve
* Fry the *soujouk*, then set aside and fry the eggs
* Fry the chives and the eggs for *bayd a toum*

Terwikat
Al' Balad

Breakfast in the Souk

My maternal grandmother, *tayta* Amineh, grew up in Tripoli during the 1940s and 50s, an ancient city known for its souks, its thriving port and century-old traditions. Her neighbourhood was close to the souks, full of lively passageways and hidden alleys, buzzing with the sound of traders, traffic and travellers.

Hidden amongst the iconic arched blue doors and black and white stone patterns of the Mameluk era, were small eateries selling Foul Medammas and Fatteh (page 58), traditional peasant-style breakfast dishes to the modest townspeople.

Young men wearing *tarboosh* hats carried large trays of small brown terracotta bowls filled to the brim with creamy, stewed fava beans and a generous pour of locally pressed virgin olive oil; others ushered out trays of deep white bowls layered with refried stale bread, chickpeas and a rich garlic, tahini yogurt sizzling like a firecracker as it's topped with hot ghee-fried nuts.

Mum would eventually walk through these same souks after school to her parents' sweet shop, picking up fresh, salty corn, from a heavy cart pushed by a local, and a warm brioche bun for afternoon tea.

Cities like Tripoli and Beirut were – and still are – a central trading place for villagers from the countryside, who would flock weekly to sell their *mouneh* – their homemade artisan pantry essentials, produced seasonally, using native crops and animal by-products. *Za'atar baladi*

(dried wild thyme), yogurt, fresh and dried cheese, dried fruit, pickled vegetables, olives and dried legumes are only some of the *mouneh* that would make its way from the paddock to the small city kitchens in homes where there was no room to grow any fresh ingredients, at the same time giving the villagers money for other things they needed from the city. *Tayta* Amineh, through the family sweet business, became a woman of influence, who was quite ahead of her time and grew very fond of such skilled artisans. She championed these relationships, and their vital role in not only sustaining traditional foods but also not having to rely on foreign imports.

Mum's weekend breakfast table is fresh and vibrant and a gentle nod to the artisans of Lebanon and their influences that *tayta* Amineh brought with her to Australia.

Left serving *salatet foul medammas*
Below preparing hummus

Fatteh
Layered Fried Bread with Chickpeas
and Yogurt

It's hard to explain what happens when
these simple ingredients come together
– you just have to try it.

200g (7oz/scant 1¼ cups) chickpeas
   (garbanzos) or 2 x 400g (14oz) cans of
   chickpeas, rinsed and drained
1 tsp bicarbonate of soda (baking soda)
2 garlic cloves
500g (1lb/2 cups) Greek yogurt
3 heaped tbsp tahini
juice of 1 lemon
3 loaves of Lebanese bread
4 tbsp ghee
1 tbsp cinnamon
35g (1¼oz/¼ cup) Lebanese pine nuts or
   slivered almonds
sea salt, to taste

Prepare the chickpeas with the
bicarbonate of soda as described on
page 22.

In a mixing bowl, crush the garlic with
a generous pinch of salt, then add the
yogurt, tahini, lemon juice and 250ml
(8½fl oz/1 cup) of water and stir to
combine until smooth, creamy and slightly
runny. Taste to make sure you are happy
with the flavour, then set aside.

Tear up the Lebanese bread into small
pieces. In a non-stick pan, heat 2
tablespoons of the ghee, then add the
bread and toss until the bread is coated,
crunchy and brown. Tip the bread out on
a flat serving plate with raised sides, then
season with some salt.

Using a slotted spoon, scoop out the
hot chickpeas from the pot, keeping
some of the liquid with them, and
scatter generously on top of the toasted
Lebanese bread. As the bread soaks up
the liquid from the chickpeas it adds
another texture to the *fatteh*.

Top the chickpeas with the yogurt mixture,
spreading it around and ensuring you
cover most of the chickpeas and bread.
Sprinkle the cinnamon on top.

Finally, in a small frying pan (skillet), heat
the remaining 2 tablespoons of ghee and
the pine nuts and fry until golden. Scatter
all over the yogurt. The ghee should sizzle
and dance on the yogurt.

Salatet Foul Medammas
Mum's Fava Bean Salad

Mum's version of *foul medammas* uses
elements of the traditional stew as part
of a fresh salad with lots of texture. If
you are planning to use dried beans and
chickpeas, you'll need to start this recipe
the night before.

250g (9oz/1½ cups) dried fava beans or
   400g (14oz) can of fava beans, rinsed
   and drained
150g (6oz/1 cup) dried chickpeas
   (garbanzos) or 1 x 400g (14oz) can of
   chickpeas, rinsed and drained
2 tsp bicarbonate of soda (baking soda),
   if using dried fava beans and dried
   chickpeas
3 garlic cloves, crushed
sea salt, to taste
½ yellow (bell) pepper, finely diced
1 small Spanish onion, finely diced
100g (3½oz/1 cup) cherry tomatoes, cut
   into quarters
a small handful of parsley, leaves removed
   and roughly chopped
a small handful of mint, leaves removed
   and roughly chopped
a small handful of fresh oregano,
   leaves removed
120ml (4fl oz/½ cup) lemon juice
120ml (4fl oz/½ cup) extra virgin olive oil,
   plus more for drizzling
zest of 1 lemon, to garnish
pomegranate seeds, to garnish

Prepare the dried fava beans and chickpeas with the bicarbonate of soda as described on pages 22 and 23.

If you are using canned fava beans and chickpeas, drain off the water and rinse well, then put in a saucepan, cover with boiling water and bring to the boil, then cover with a lid and simmer for 10 minutes.

Place the crushed garlic and a pinch of salt in a mixing bowl and add the fava beans and chickpeas. Add the chopped vegetables and fresh herbs along with the lemon juice and extra virgin olive oil. Toss the salad well and serve immediately in a wide bowl with plenty of lemon zest, oil and pomegranate seeds.

Hummus bi Tahini w' Lahme
Hummus Topped with Spiced Minced Lamb

Use course mince here, as the flecks of fat caramelize in the ghee and add deliciously rich savoury tones to this silky hummus.

350g (12oz/2 cups) dried chickpeas (garbanzos)
1 tsp bicarbonate of soda (baking soda)
250g (9oz/generous 1 cup) tahini
100ml (3½fl oz/scant ½ cup) lemon juice
3 garlic cloves
50–100ml (2–3fl oz/¼–scant ½ cup) ice-cold water
sea salt, to taste

For the meat topping
500g (1lb 2oz) coarse minced (ground) lamb
1 tsp Sabaa Bharat (page 20)
½ tsp ground cinnamon
2 tbsp ghee
75g (2½oz/¼ cup) pine nuts

For the garnish
1 tsp paprika

Prepare the chickpeas with the bicarbonate of soda as described on page 22, extending the cooking time by 15 minutes, or until the chickpeas collapse easily but are not yet mushy.

Allow the chickpeas to cool slightly, but drain while still warm, reserve 3–4 tablespoons of the chickpeas to garnish, then transfer the rest to a food processor and blitz until a stiff paste forms. Remove the lid of the processor and give it a mix, then put the lid back on. With the machine running, gradually add the tahini, lemon juice and garlic, and salt to taste. Once those ingredients have been processed and while the machine is still running, add the ice-cold water, drizzling slowly, and keep processing the hummus for another 3 minutes.

If you have made this in advance, place the hummus in the fridge once it has cooled, then bring back to room temperature when you wish to serve, otherwise set aside until required.

Heat a wide-based frying pan (skillet) on a high heat, add the minced meat and begin to break down the meat with a wooden spoon. Continue to cook the meat until all the liquid has evaporated, add the spices and 1 tablespoon of the ghee and continue to toss on the heat until the ghee has melted, the meat has caramelized and the spices have been incorporated.

In a small frying pan (skillet), heat the remaining tablespoon of ghee along with the pine nuts and fry until they are golden brown. Add the pine nuts straight to the minced meat and combine them evenly throughout.

To assemble, place the hummus on a flat plate and spread it out evenly. Tip the minced meat on top and spread over the hummus. Garnish with the reserved whole chickpeas and the paprika.

Salatet Bayd w' Batata

Egg and Potato Breakfast Salad

This is a quick and easy dish that really only calls for salt, *bharat* and good-quality extra virgin olive oil.

6 eggs
500g (1lb 2oz) baby new potatoes
a handful of oregano leaves
a handful of mint
a handful of parsley
1 small Spanish onion
sea salt, to taste
¼ tsp freshly ground pepper
½ tsp Aleppo chilli
¼ tbsp Sabaa Bharat (page 20)
60ml (2fl oz/¼ cup) extra virgin olive oil
a squeeze of lemon
1 small chilli, finely sliced (optional)

Put the eggs in a medium-sized saucepan with enough water to cover. Bring the water to the boil and, once boiling, place the lid on the pan and boil for 30 seconds. Turn off the heat and put your timer on for 12 minutes, for hard-boiled eggs. Once cool enough, peel the shells and set aside.

While the eggs are cooking, wash the potatoes, place them whole into a pot of water and bring to the boil, then turn down the heat and leave to simmer, covered, for 15 minutes. Test with a sharp knife to see if they are soft and cooked through. Remove from the heat and drain.

While the eggs and potatoes are cooking, finely chop the herbs and onions and place in a mixing bowl.

Cut the potatoes in half if small, and quarters if slightly larger and place in the mixing bowl. Cut the eggs in quarters and add them to the bowl, seasoning well with salt, pepper, Aleppo chilli and *bharat*, then add the oil and lemon and combine with your hands gently so as not to break up the ingredients too much. To serve, place the salad into a serving dish and garnish with a drizzle of oil and the fresh chilli.

Jazz this up with extra fresh green herbs and Aleppo chilli for added texture and to complement a breakfast spread.

Labne bil Zeit
Strained Yogurt Balls

These can be prepared in advance and preserved in oil. Mum assembles them on a plate and has a few bowls set up with different toppings: sumac, Aleppo chilli, and my favourite, a mix of za'atar and roasted pistachio.

2kg (2lb 4oz) plain yogurt
1 tbsp sea salt
neutral oil, as needed
olive oil, as needed
50g (2½oz/½ cup) Aleppo chilli (if you cannot find Aleppo chilli, use chilli flakes and smoked paprika)
50g (2½oz/½ cup) sumac
50g (2½oz/½ cup) Za'atar Halabi (page 22) or Za'atar Baladi (page 20)
40g (1½oz/¼ cup) roasted pistachios, finely chopped
50g (1¾oz/½ cup) roasted walnuts
25g (1oz) fresh chives, washed well and finely chopped

Mix the yogurt with the salt, before pouring it into a colander or sieve lined with a muslin (cheesecloth) and bring the edges together. Fold the cloth over the yogurt and place over a bowl for the liquid to strain from the yogurt; put this in the fridge.

Leave this for 24–36 hours, removing the water from the bowl each time you check to make sure the yogurt is draining freely. Leave until most of the liquid has dripped into the bowl and the yogurt is thicker and fairly dry. (Depending on the type of yogurt, this may take longer.)

Take your strained *labne* from the cloth and spoon out enough to make a small ball in your hand. Roll it around and place it in a container with 2–3 clean cloths underneath to continue to drain and dry it out. Repeat for the rest of the *labne*. If the *labne* is still too wet to handle, just spoon it out and place it straight onto the cloth and into the fridge to continue to dry out for a few hours. Once dry, it will be easier to handle.

Place the balls in a jar or container half filled with neutral oil and olive oil, and keep them in the fridge for up to 2 months.

Set up bowls of each of the toppings and, to serve, place the oiled *labne* balls in each and roll around to coat. Any remaining coated *labne* balls will last up to a week in the fridge.

Below *fatteh*
Right serving *labne bil zeit*

Several weeks before
* If you are making the *kabees* and *makdous* (page 26–30) you will have to do so when they are in season and allow several weeks to pickle, otherwise purchase from a Mediterranean or Middle Eastern grocer

Several days before
* Strain the yogurt to make the *labne*
* Make *labne* into balls, as per the recipe, and store in a glass container in the fridge

Two days before
* Wash and soak the chickpeas and fava beans
* Break up the Lebanese bread for the *fatteh*, and set aside in an airtight bag in the fridge
* Wash all the fresh herbs and fresh vegetables, dry well and pack in an airtight container in the fridge

The day before (place all in the fridge in an airtight container)
* Boil the chickpeas, leave to cool
* Make the hummus, leave to cool
* Boil the fava beans, leave to cool
* Make the garlic tahini yogurt for the *fatteh*
* Prepare all toppings for the *labne* station

In the morning
* Reheat the chickpeas and fava beans
* Bring out the hummus to come to room temperature
* Boil the eggs and potatoes
* Fry and season the mince, then set aside
* Set up the *labne* station: take the *labne* out of the fridge 20 minutes before serving, as the oil will have solidified
* Chop the ingredients for the fava bean salad
* Chop the ingredients for the egg salad
* Fry the bread pieces with ghee and set aside to assemble the *fatteh* just before serving
* Have a small frying pan (skillet) ready with pine nuts and ghee to use on both the *fatteh* and hummus when serving
* Plate the hummus and add the reheated meat
* Assemble the *foul* salad, then set aside
* Assemble the egg and potato salad, then set aside
* Assemble a pickle platter, as opposite
* Turn the heat on for the pine nuts and ghee
* Assemble the *fatteh*, add a sprinkle of cinnamon and finally the ghee and pine nuts, then eat immediately

Mansaf Al' Eid

Lamb for Eid

When I think of Mum's lamb *mansaf*, a glorious meaty centrepiece amongst an assembly of complementary sides, I immediately think of Eid. While lamb cuts and mince are the main meat used by Lebanese people when cooking *tabikh* (stews and casseroles) during the week, whole animals as well as cuts of shoulder and leg are reserved for the feasts of the weekend, religious celebrations and special occasions.

To mark the end of Ramadan, Mum would gather close friends and family and we would indulge in a spread of *mansaf kharouf*: whole lamb shoulder, tender meat falling off the bone, on a bed of fluffy, spiced rice, adorned with fried nuts and currants.

Eid al Fitr is a celebration that marks the end of Ramadan for Muslims around the world. Buying a whole sheep, lamb or goat, at least for those who could afford it, to slaughter and give to the less fortunate, was an act of praise and reverence to mark the end of the year's fasting.

For Eid al Adha, celebration of the sacrifice, many like my *jido* (grandfather), who had the means, would slaughter one animal per child he had (and that was 15, remember), and have the meat distributed all over the poorer regions of Tripoli. Mum always said he was a very generous man and would feed the whole of Tripoli if he could. He never forgot the poverty he was born into and lucky enough to escape. I was too young to ask or notice, but I often wonder how he dealt with the heartbreak of leaving Tripoli, a man who was part of the fabric of society and a city that flowed through his veins. When he migrated, he spent a lot of time at the local mosque, walking for thirty minutes from home every Friday morning, prayer beads turning through his fingers. There, a group slowly formed of men who knew him or knew of him from his past life, finding solace between holy walls and in shared experiences, thousands of miles away from home.

Mum's spreads almost always consisted of a salad – seasonal, crunchy, vibrant, tossed in a rich and delicately balanced dressing. *Fattoush* not only renews the palate between mouthfuls of lamb and rice, it creates something I like to call plate juices that become one with the flavours of the other dishes, to be mopped up with that last piece of bread and make the final mouthfuls delectable. Although it began as a feast for Eid, this spread was so popular, it slowly became a weekend treat and will always hold a special place in my heart, as it was the first spread we created for our Sunday Kitchen sessions. The lamb, after very little preparation, basically cooks itself and is a real crowd-pleaser.

Frakeh
Ground Meat with Fine Bulgur Wheat and Southern Spices

A version of the southern-style Kibbeh Nayyeh (page 116), this *frakeh* is fresh, spicy and aromatic, remarkably different to that of the north, mainly because of the hero ingredient, *kammouneh* – a dry, bold spice blend rich in cumin and mixed with rose petals, marjoram, mint, cinnamon, cloves and black pepper. *Kibbeh* is not regular minced (ground) meat. It is like a lean paste so fresh it can be eaten raw. You will need to go to a Lebanese butcher and let them know what you are cooking.

1 small brown onion, quartered
2 spring onions (scallions), white and
   green parts, trimmed and quartered
¼ red (bell) pepper, deseeded
130g (4½oz/¾ cup) fine brown bulgur
   wheat
1 long red chilli (optional)
1 sprig of basil, leaves removed
1 sprig of mint, leaves removed
1 sprig of marjoram
½ tbsp Sabaa Bharat (page 20)
½ tbsp ground cumin
1 heaped tbsp Kammouneh (page 20)
500g (1lb 4oz) ground *kibbeh* mince
   (combination of beef and lamb)
sea salt, to taste

To serve
extra virgin olive oil, as needed
1 bunch of fresh mint
1 bunch of fresh radish roots
1 bunch of spring onions (scallions), roots
   removed and stems cut down
fresh chilli, sliced (optional)

In a food processor, add the onions, red pepper, bulgur wheat and chilli, along with the herbs and spices and salt to taste. Pulse for 30 seconds until combined and moist but not runny. The aim is to form a loose and crumbly mixture that will be used to flavour the meat as well as to garnish.

Reserve about 80g (3oz/½ cup) of the loose bulgur wheat mixture and put the rest with the *kibbeh* meat in a large bowl. Make sure your hands are washed well, and have a small bowl of cold water beside you to help with the stickiness of the fresh meat. (Note that the water is not an ingredient but an aid and should be used sparingly.)

Begin to combine the meat and bulgur wheat mixture together, incorporating both as much as possible without leaving any parts of the meat unflavoured. Aim to complete this process as quickly as possible, as when handling raw meat it should be done with the least amount of contact. The mixture should not be sticky or too wet.

Once you have thoroughly combined the meat and bulgur wheat mixture, using a slightly wet hand, break off a piece the size of half your palm, then shape this by clenching your fist slightly to create finger indentations (see opposite). Repeat with the remaining mixture, garnish with the reserved bulgur wheat mixture.

Finish with a generous drizzle of extra virgin olive oil and serve with a platter of fresh mint, radish, spring onions and chilli. Enjoy with Lebanese bread between mouthfuls of fresh vegetables.

Below preparing *frakeh*

For the Lebanese diaspora, migrating to Australia involved meeting and mixing with Lebanese people from different regions, and so began the exchanging of recipes and cooking styles.

Mansaf Kharouf
Lamb on a Bed of Jewelled Rice

Serving lamb on a bed of rice is popular all over the Levant, with each region preparing it slightly differently. A longer-grain rice, Sella rice, is usually preferred as it is less starchy and cooks beautifully with the broth, ensuring the grains remain fluffy. Adorning this rice with nuts and currants is really up to your taste. The currants add a refreshing sweetness.

Lebanese families forge a strong allegiance to their butcher, and ours has been the same through three generations. Mum always buys lamb on the bone and asks the butcher to cut the shoulder to fit her casserole dish (Dutch oven) and trim off as much fat as possible. You could adapt the recipe to a small cut of lamb shoulder; or, if you buy meat off the bone, add a lamb shank to the pot.

Slow-cooking on the bone is a common practice in Lebanese cooking and adds a depth of flavour to the nutritious broth, which can be used to cook the rice. Trimming excess fat gives a flavoursome broth that is both light and clear yet rich and layered with flavour. Too much fat will spoil the dish. As she did when we were young, Mum always ladles a few spoons of broth into a bowl with a generous squeeze of lemon juice for us to drink and drizzle over the meat and rice.

1 whole lamb shoulder, cleaned of fat and
   cut into quarters (ask your butcher to
   do this)

For the marinade
1 tbsp Sabaa Bharat (page 20)
½ tbsp paprika
sea salt, to taste
1 tsp ground black pepper
120ml (4fl oz/½ cup) olive oil

Aromatics for the stock
1 cinnamon stick
4 dried bay leaves
6 cardamom pods
2 star anise
2 dried limes
6 allspice berries

For the rice
720g (1lb 9½oz/4 cups) Indian basmati
   rice (parboiled Sella if available,
   otherwise regular basmati is fine)
1 tbsp ghee
½ tsp black pepper
1 tsp Sabaa Bharat (page 20)
sea salt, to taste
6 cloves
1.4 litres (50fl oz/6 cups) meat stock
   (from cooking the lamb shoulder)
60g (2oz/½ cup) currants

For the nuts
2 tbsp ghee
75g (2½oz/½ cup) halved almonds
60g (2oz/½ cup) cashews
40g (1½oz/¼ cup) pine nuts

Put the trimmed lamb in a large mixing bowl. Add the marinade spices and olive oil and massage it well.

Place a large, heavy-based, flameproof casserole dish (Dutch oven) on a high heat, add 3 litres (100fl oz/12 cups) of water and bring to the boil. Add the aromatics for the stock and keep it boiling.

Place a large saucepan on a high heat. Take each piece of shoulder one at a time and let it sizzle for 3 minutes on each side until it forms a golden brown crust all around and you begin to see juices form in the pan. Once you sear each piece of lamb, place it directly in the large stock pot with the aromatics and boiling water. It is not important if you miss sections of the meat, just as long as most of it is seared.

Once you have browned all the meat, ladle one cup of the stock into the pan and stir in all the juices and pieces of meat before returning it to the casserole with the meat. Make sure the meat is completely submerged. If not, add more boiling water.

Bring the pot to the boil, uncovered, and skim off and discard any foamy scum that rises to the top. Reduce the heat until the water is boiling very gently, put the lid on and let it cook for up to 3 hours.

After 1 hour, use a knife to poke the limes to release their flavour. Remove any extra scum that rises during the first hour; the aim is to get the stock as clean as possible during the cooking process. The meat is ready when it is very soft and tender and falling off the bone when lifted from the pot. This is when you can use the stock for the jewelled rice. Turn the heat off, and bring back to the boil to reheat later, if necessary.

Wash the rice as described on page 23. Place a deep (non-stick) saucepan on a high heat and heat the ghee until melted, add the rice and stir gently to coat it in the ghee. It's really important you season your rice before adding any liquid, so add the spices and salt, followed by the cloves and then the stock.

Bring the pot to a boil, then turn down the heat, cover and simmer on low for 40–50 minutes, or until the rice is cooked through. Turn off the heat and leave covered to cool down slightly.

To prepare the nuts, place the ghee in a small frying pan (skillet) and fry the nuts one type at a time, in batches, until lightly golden and fragrant. The nuts cook at different times and temperatures so keep an eye on them and stir constantly. Once browned, remove with a slotted spoon and place in a bowl.

Once the rice has slightly cooled, scoop it onto a large serving dish, with elevated sides – not too deep but deep enough so that the rice doesn't spill out. Add half of the nuts and currants and lightly toss them through the rice.

Using tongs, gently pull the meat out of the pot and lay the tender pieces all over the rice, pulling some of the larger chunks apart. I like to keep some of the meat pieces on the bone.

Adorn the meat with the rest of the nuts and currants and serve immediately.

Left and below *mansaf kharouf*

Tabbouch w' Khobez Mekli

Mum's Aubergine and Yogurt Dip with Fried Bread Crackers

While Baba Ghanouj (page 183) is popular for its smokiness, it is an acquired taste and one we didn't love as children. Mum created her signature dip instead; she fried the aubergine and combined it with a garlic and mint yogurt, and, at home, we know this as 'Tabbouch dip'.

8 medium-sized aubergines (eggplants)
  – seedless variety, with dark black skin
  and bright green tops
sea salt
neutral oil, for deep-frying
3 garlic cloves
500g (1lb 2oz/2 cups) Greek yogurt
1½ tbsp crushed dried mint, plus ½ tbsp
  to garnish

For the bread crackers (*khobez mekli*)
5 whole pieces of Lebanese bread
2 tbsp Za'atar Baladi (page 20)
a handful of oregano leaves (optional)

It is crucial to draw out the liquid from the aubergines with salt before frying. They must be prepared on the day so start by washing them and removing the tops.

Remove the skin of the aubergines, leaving a few thin strips of skin around (like a zebra pattern), as the skin adds texture. Cut the aubergines in half lengthways, then in quarters so you have 4 boats. Chop into large cubes and place in a strainer.

Place the strainer over a bowl and add a large handful of salt. Leave, uncovered, overnight in the fridge.

Tear the bread into large palm-sized pieces. The inner side of the bread is coarse and that is the side that should be face down when frying. Place a colander over a bowl beside the stove.

Heat up a medium-sized frying pan or wok and add 500ml (17fl oz/2 cups) of oil. Once the oil is hot, reduce to a medium heat, add one piece of bread to test the frying time and colour. Once you place the bread in the oil, tap on each corner to stop it from curling up. The colour of the bread should be golden when it leaves the oil and then usually darkens to a light brown once it has cooled down. Once you get the hang of it, you can start frying in batches of 4, but be mindful not to overcrowd the pan. Leave the bread crackers to cool down and any excess oil to drip off in the prepared colander.

In the same pan, add more oil and begin to fry the aubergines in small batches for about 10 minutes until they are a browned on the outside and soft on the inside. Place the fried aubergines in a colander to strain any excess oil further. Leave the aubergines to drain for at least 2 hours.

To prepare the yogurt, place the garlic and a generous pinch of salt in a pestle and mortar and crush before transferring to a mixing bowl. Add the yogurt, using a wooden spoon and beat the yogurt with the garlic and salt mixture. Once combined, mix in the crushed dried mint. Taste and add more salt or garlic if necessary.

Once the aubergines have drained, tear them slightly with your fingers into the yogurt mixture, and then combine until you have a thick and textured dip.

To serve, place the fried bread crackers on a platter and generously sprinkle the za'atar all over, and fresh oregano if you like. Garnish the dip with dried mint and serve alongside the fried bread crackers.

Arnabeet Mekli w' Tarator
Fried Cauliflower and Rustic Tarator

Mum's *tarator* has a large handful of finely chopped parsley tossed through it, which gives it a freshness and a rustic texture that works so well against the fried cauliflower. Although traditionally the *tarator* is served in a small bowl beside the cauliflower; we like to drizzle it all over the pile of golden fried florets and scatter with a generous pinch of Aleppo pepper for an extra smoky crunch.

2 large heads of cauliflower
neutral oil, for frying (your choice)

For the rustic tarator
1 large garlic clove
sea salt, to taste
4 heaped tbsp tahini
juice of 1 lemon
½ bunch of parsley
Aleppo pepper, to garnish
fresh Lebanese bread, to serve

Wash the cauliflower heads and trim the florets, keeping their stems attached. Place the florets in a pot of water seasoned with salt and bring to the boil. Boil for 5 minutes, then drain and set aside.

Fill a frying pan (skillet) or wok with any neutral oil, and bring to a high heat before reducing slightly. Add a handful of cauliflower florets, being mindful not to overcrowd the pan and turning them continuously as they cook. Fry until the cauliflower is a rich golden brown. Remove from the oil and place on a plate covered with paper towels to remove excess oil. Repeat with the remaining cauliflower.

To make the *tarator*, crush the garlic with salt in a small bowl. Add the tahini, being mindful to scoop from the bottom of the jar to ensure you are not just using the oil at the top. Begin to break in the tahini with the garlic, adding the lemon juice to avoid it from curdling and stiffening. You can also add water and use a whisk to reach a desired consistency.

Prepare the parsley by washing well and removing the stems, then finely chopping the leaves. Add the parsley and combine.

Place the fried cauliflower on a flat plate and drizzle the *tarator* all over. Garnish with Aleppo pepper and serve with fresh Lebanese bread.

Deluxe Fattoush
Deluxe Salad

Mum loves to joke that the *fattoush* of her childhood consisted of no more than four vegetables and relied on what was in season in the garden or whatever she could find in the fridge. I am completely responsible for the exaggeration of the ingredients here.

3 Lebanese cucumbers
3 tomatoes
½ yellow (bell) pepper
½ red (bell) pepper
5 spring onions (scallions)
1 bunch of small radishes
1 cos lettuce
¼ small white cabbage
¼ small purple cabbage
½ bunch of mint
1 bunch of parsley
1 bunch of purslane (if available)
1 bunch of oregano
1 loaf of Lebanese bread
1 pomegranate, deseeded

For the dressing
60ml (2fl oz/¼ cup) pomegranate molasses (or to taste)
120ml (4fl oz/½ cup) lemon juice
120ml (4fl oz/½ cup) olive oil
sea salt, to taste
1 tbsp sumac, plus extra for serving
2 garlic cloves, crushed

Wash all the vegetables and fresh herbs and leave them to dry.

I like to remove the leaves from the stems of fresh herbs and keep them whole, that way I can taste each herb in each mouthful. Preparing the *fattoush* can be done the day before (minus the tomatoes, which I like to dice fresh on the day) and kept in an airtight container in the fridge, along with the dressing in a jar.

Dice the cucumbers, tomatoes, peppers and spring onions to size; keep this a consistent 1cm (½in). Chop the radishes into discs and then matchsticks, like a julienne. The cos lettuce can also be chopped in 1cm (½in) lengths. Using a sharp knife, finely slice the cabbages, start from the tip of the wedge and work your way around, keeping the slices thin and consistent.

Pick off the leaves of the mint, parsley, purslane, if using, and oregano and set aside in a bowl. If the mint leaves are large, cut them in half, too.

If you do not want to fry the bread, you can place it in the oven at 180°C/350°F (gas 6) and bake it until crisp, then lightly crush with your hands into a bowl to garnish the *fattoush*. If you are frying the bread as part of the spread, then by all means crush with your hands to garnish at the end.

In a small mixing bowl, combine the dressing ingredients and mix well with a fork.

To assemble, toss half the pomegranate seeds with all the remaining ingredients, except for the bread, with the dressing, and combine using your hands. Scoop the salad into a serving bowl. Scatter the crushed Lebanese bread on top along with the remaining pomegranate seeds and an extra pinch of sumac. Serve immediately.

The day before
* Prepare the aubergines by salting generously and placing in a strainer overnight
* Prepare and trim the lamb fat to begin cooking first thing in the morning
* Wash the *fattoush* ingredients and leave to dry, then store in an airtight bag in the fridge
* Fry the Lebanese bread, cool, then store in an airtight bag, reserving the oil for the aubergines the following day
* Make the *tarator*, chop the parsley, cover separately and set aside in the fridge
* Prepare the *kammouneh* crumb, then set aside in an airtight container in the fridge.
* Prepare the cauliflower, boil, then leave to cool and place in an airtight container in the fridge
* Fry the nuts, leave to cool, then place in an airtight container
* Deseed the pomegranate and store in an airtight container in the fridge

In the morning (4 hours before lunch)
* Sear the lamb, place in a pot on the stove and begin cooking
* Prepare the fresh vegetables for the platter alongside the *frakeh*
* Fry the aubergines and leave to drain
* Fry the cauliflower and leave to drain
* Chop the *fattoush* ingredients and make the dressing, then set aside in the fridge
* Make the aubergine dip and set aside in the fridge
* Prepare the rice using the stock from the lamb pot

Final stages
* Garnish the fried bread and assemble on a platter to serve
* Combine the *kibbeh* meat and *kammouneh*, assemble the *frakeh*, plate and garnish
* Plate the fresh vegetable platter
* Plate the aubergine and yogurt dip ready to serve
* Plate the cauliflower, mix the *tarator* and drizzle on top to garnish
* Combine the *fattoush* with the dressing, plate and garnish
* Plate up the rice with the meat on top, garnish with the nuts and currants

Ma'koulate
Al' Bahar

By the Sea

El Mina, which means 'the harbour', is the charming port
of Tripoli. The city wakes to the banter of the fisherman,
who work tirelessly on small boats, preparing their
catch for the markets, and restaurateurs who arrive
early to get the first and best pick. The afternoon
sings a different tune, with people flocking from all
over Al Shmaal (the North) to walk along the *corniche*
(seashore walk) and enjoy the fresh air.

As a child, Mum remembers the humble food vendors, crammed within the four kilometres of the *corniche*, selling everything from fresh, hot, salty corn, *balila* (broad beans), *termos* (freshly boiled lupini beans), freshly roasted peanuts, and *bizer* (roasted pumpkin seeds), ready to delight the daily visitors who would sit for hours with friends and neighbours as if time stood still.

Although busy and often loud, the harbour was a haven for my grandmother, Amineh, who made the 20-minute commute several times a week, always sitting close to her favourite vendor, her legs aching from the day's work, as she took in the salty air and watched the sun set. She worked tirelessly in the hope of acquiring a small house in front of the port of El Mina, where she eventually retired. But the civil war in 1975 altered everyone's hopes, dreams and desires.

Samkeh Harra w' Sayadiyeh (page 92), although eaten all over Lebanon, are two dishes specific to El Mina, where long queues formed at tiny hole-in-the wall vendors to buy their fried fish stuffed into a fresh wrap and filled with fried potatoes, tabbouleh, pickles and spicy tahini sauce.

When I make this spread, I am reminded of Mum's kitchen, the sweet aroma of the onions caramelizing to form the stock for the rice, one that lingers for a few days, the aubergines charring on the gas stove and two large bunches of parsley calling out to be picked and finely chopped into *tabbouleh*. Cooking often happened both inside and outside the kitchen, for speed but also to avoid the persistent smell of fried fish. Two outdoor gas cookers take care of the frying and make sure everything is hot and ready at the same time.

Samkeh Harra w' Sayadiyeh
Spicy Fish and Golden Fisherman's Rice

For this recipe, I use medium to large white-fleshed fish such as snapper, bream or blue-eyed cod – choose something you can find locally. The rice can seem overwhelming to prepare but is well worth the effort.

For the sayadiyeh
head, tail and bones removed and
  reserved from the whole fish below
1 tablespoon salt, plus more to taste
1 tablespoon paprika
olive oil, as needed
4 medium-sized brown onions
neutral oil, of choice
500g (1lb 2oz) white-flesh fish fillets,
  such as snapper or bream
540g (1lb 3oz/3 cups) medium-grain rice

For the samkeh harra
4 garlic cloves, crushed
4 heaped tbsp tahini
juice of 1 lemon
1 heaped tbsp Greek yogurt
about 2 tbsp smoked paprika
½ tsp chilli powder (or to taste)
1 bunch of coriander (cilantro),
  finely chopped
3kg (6lb 10oz) whole fish, cleaned,
  filleted with the skin on (head, tail and
  bones removed and reserved for the
  sayadiyeh)
olive oil, as needed
sea salt, to taste

To garnish
150g (5oz/1½ cups) walnuts
3 tbsp neutral oil
50g (2oz/⅓ cup) pine nuts
50g (2oz/⅓ cup) halved almonds
40g (1½oz/⅓ cup) cashews
½ pomegranate, deseeded (page 31)

Unless you are familiar with cleaning, gutting and filleting fish, ask your fishmonger to do it for you, but make sure you ask for the head, tails and bones in a separate bag.

To make the sayadiyeh (golden fisherman's rice), preheat the oven to 180°C/350°F (gas 6) and rinse the fish carcass (head, tail and bones) under cold running water quickly to remove any bloodied bits, then place on a heavy-based, flameproof, ovenproof dish and massage with salt, paprika and 125ml (4fl oz/½ cup) olive oil. Bake for about 30 minutes or until the skin is crisp and caramelized. There should be no moisture present, just a caramelized crust that has formed on the base of the dish. It is this crust that you will build on for the flavour of the rice.

Meanwhile, dice the onions finely and set aside. Heat a wok on the stove and add 250ml (8½fl oz/1 cup) of oil. While the oil heats up, salt the white-flesh fish fillets well and begin to fry them for about 4 minutes on each side until golden brown. Place the fried fillets on a plate with a paper towel to drain some of the oil and set aside for garnishing the sayadiyeh later. Add another cup of oil to the wok, leave it to heat up, then add the onions and fry until they are caramelized and very dark brown in colour; they should be removed just before they begin to burn. The darker the onions, the sweeter they become and the more flavoursome the rice is. Once the onions have cooked, add them to the dish with the fish bones using a slotted spoon (discard the oil) along with 1.4 litres (50fl oz/6 cups) of water. Place this on the stove top over a high heat and leave to boil until the onions soften, about 10 minutes, dissolving any crust that has formed and ensuring it is now in the liquid. This is the stock you will use to cook the rice. Remove and discard the head, tail and any large bones.

Wash the rice as described on page 23.

Put the rice in a large non-stick saucepan and place on a low heat. Place a large strainer over the pot and tip all the onions and stock into the strainer. Using a wooden spoon, push through as much as you can to enhance the flavour of the rice. Discard whatever remains. Mix the stock with the rice. There should be enough liquid to cover the rice by 1cm (½in). Adjust if there isn't enough by adding 120–250ml (4–8½fl oz/½–1 cup) of boiling water. Season with salt, bring to the boil and simmer for 20 minutes before mixing the rice with a wooden spoon to ensure it doesn't caramelize and stick to the base of the pan. Leave to cook for a further 15 minutes, or until tender.

For the *samkeh harra* (spicy fish), begin by crushing the garlic and a generous pinch of salt. Put them in a large mixing bowl. Gradually add the tahini and the lemon juice, beating quickly to break down the tahini and stop it from becoming stiff (you can also add some water here to help). Add the yogurt, 1 teaspoon of the paprika and the chilli powder and combine, before finally adding 1 litre (34fl oz/4 cups) of water. Stir in the finely chopped coriander, using a small whisk to mix and break up any clumps that may form. Taste and adjust the salt and garlic to your preference; the mixture should have a strong hint of lemon. Place the tahini mixture into the fridge as you prepare your fish.

Preheat the oven to 180°C/350°F (gas 6). To prepare your filleted whole fish, place the fish (skin-side down) in a heavy-based ovenproof dish and massage with 1 tablespoon salt, 1 tablespoon paprika and 125ml (4fl oz/½ cup) olive oil (rubbing olive oil on the base as well). Place the ovenproof dish on your stove top over a high heat and allow the fish skin to sear. Do not flip the fish over, just remove from the heat once the edges have started to take colour and the fillets have puffed up and look slightly raised. Pour the tahini mixture over the fish and bake in the preheated oven for about 25–30 minutes. The cooking time may vary depending on the size and thickness. The fish will poach

in the water and you will be left with a slightly thickened tahini sauce. If you feel it's too thick, which can happen with some types of tahini, add a cup of water around the edges while baking, to loosen up slightly. Shake the pan to distribute the water. The tahini sauce should thicken and reduce slightly.

While the fish is cooking, fry the walnuts in the neutral oil until they turn a golden colour, then, using a slotted spoon, remove from the pan and set aside to cool. Using the same oil, repeat with the pine nuts, almonds and cashews, ensuring you cook each type on its own. Set aside.

To serve the *samkeh harra*, leave the baked fish to stand for 5 minutes before garnishing. Crush the walnuts with your hands and scatter all over the fish, along with the pomegranate seeds.

To serve the *sayadiyeh*, transfer the rice to a large serving dish and flake and scatter the reserved fried fish fillets on top followed by the rest of the fried nuts. Serve immediately.

Below onions caramelizing
for the *sayadiyeh*
Right *samkeh harra*

For the *sayadiyeh*, the darker the onions,
the sweeter they taste.

Left and below *samak mekli*

Sivine's Tabbouleh
A Guide to the Best Tabbouleh

There is an endless debate amongst Lebanese mothers as to whether the parsley should be picked and chopped before it is washed and dried, and vice versa. Both work perfectly well, in my opinion, and we children usually inherit our mother's method.

Another great tabbouleh debate is whether to soak the bulgur wheat in water before adding it to the salad, or place it on top of the tomatoes to absorb their juices. I do the latter, sifting the bulgur to remove any impurities before adding it to the tomatoes. It's also a good idea to finely chop the small brown onion, and toss the *bharat* through it before adding it to the *tabbouleh*, to kill the harshness of the raw onion in the salad.

6 bunches of flat-leaf parsley
  (see method)
1 bunch of mint, leaves picked and
  finely chopped
6 tomatoes, finely chopped
80g (3oz/½ cup) fine brown bulgur wheat
1 bunch of spring onions (scallions)
  (about 8 stems), finely chopped
1 very small brown onion, finely chopped
1 tsp Sabaa Bharat (page 20)
250ml (8½fl oz/1 cup) extra virgin olive oil
250ml (8½fl oz/1 cup) lemon juice
sea salt, to taste
baby cos leaves or iceberg lettuce cups,
  to serve
zest of 1 lemon

Start by washing your parsley well in a large mixing bowl, changing the water several times. Mum hangs bunches on the washing line to allow it to dry completely before sorting the leaves from the stems.

Avoid removing the stems completely as they serve as a handle for when you are picking. Break off the smaller stems from the larger one and concentrate on putting the leaves as close together as possible. A few bits of stem here and there are fine.

Once you are ready to finely chop the parsley, hold the bunch from the leaves and cut off the stems on the chopping board in one swift motion. With a firm grip on the bunch of leaves, begin by chopping them firmly in a straight line almost trying to achieve long narrow strips. This is tricky to do the first time but becomes easier. Do not use a food processor for this.

Use a large stainless steel mixing bowl for this. Place the parsley and mint to one side of the bowl, place the tomatoes to another side, add the bulgur wheat on top and massage to allow it to expand and soften in the juices from the tomatoes. Add the spring onions and brown onion to one side of the bowl and add the *bharat*, also massaging through the onions. Leave to rest for 15 minutes. This leads me to my next matriarchal tip: tabbouleh should always be mixed with clean hands and never utensils; this ensures you can gently combine the ingredients with the dressing and feel the ingredients have married well.

The measurements for the perfect tabbouleh dressing are usually equal parts lemon juice to extra virgin olive oil, added intuitively and to taste. One person is the designated pourer, usually one of my daughters, and I do the mixing. Wash your hands well, pour the extra virgin olive oil onto the salad and begin to mix the ingredients with your hands, adding the lemon juice and salt before tasting with a spoon; it should have a punchy lemon flavour so adjust the lemon and oil until you are satisfied that the flavours are well balanced. The tabbouleh should be juicy and not dry.

To serve, lay the lettuce cups around a platter with a rim and mount the tabbouleh into the middle. Finally, zest the lemon on top of the tabbouleh.

Tabbouleh sits proudly in the middle of our table almost every Sunday lunchtime.

Samak Mekli w' Tarator
Fried Fish with a Tahini Sauce

Almost every weekend in season, we enjoy my father-in-law, Naji's, freshly caught fish along with stories of the ones that got away! Often the larger fish are reserved for baking and the smaller ones are floured, generously salted and fried whole until the skin is crispy and the flesh soft and tender.

1kg (2lb 4oz) whiting (about 10 fish)
125g (4oz/1 cup) plain (all-purpose) flour
about 1 tbsp salt
neutral oil, for frying
1 lemon, for zest and wedges, to serve
1 quantity of Tarator (page 80), made
    without parsley and with a pinch of
    Aleppo chilli, to serve
flaky sea salt, to taste

Whiting are fried whole and eaten whole, except for the long bone in the centre. Ask your fishmonger to remove the scales and clean the fish for you. You will still need to run the fish under cold running water and remove any bloody bits.

Pat the fish dry with a paper towel to remove any excess moisture, lightly salt the inside of the small fish with your fingers and set aside.

In a mixing bowl, mix the flour with 1 tbsp salt, then set aside.

Heat a large frying pan (skillet) or wok with neutral oil, enough to submerge a whole fish. As it begins to heat up, place each fish in the salted flour and coat well on both sides.

Place the fish into the hot oil and cook on both sides until golden brown. Don't overcrowd the pan. Remove the fish when it is cooked and place on a plate with paper towels to drain any excess oil.

Zest the lemon on top of the fish and serve with the lemon wedges and *tarator*, and season with flaky sea salt.

Salatet Batenjan w' Khobez Mekli
Aubergine Dip and Fried Lebanese Bread

This smoky aubergine dip is the perfect side to complement the rich tahini in the *samkeh harra*.

4 medium-sized seedless aubergines
    (eggplants), washed
2 garlic cloves, crushed
100g (4oz/1 cup) cherry tomatoes,
    washed and cut into quarters
1 long green chilli, thinly sliced
1 small Spanish onion, finely diced
½ yellow (bell pepper), finely diced
½ bunch of fresh oregano leaves, chopped
½ pomegranate, deseeded (page 31)
juice and zest of 1 lemon
3 tbsp extra virgin olive oil
sea salt, to taste
Khobez Mekli (page 78), to serve

Ideally use an exposed flame to char the aubergine skin, over a barbecue or on a gas stove. Or, you can use the oven on maximum for 45 minutes; you will achieve the texture but not the smoky flavour.

Using a knife poke the aubergines all over, then place directly over the flame and rotate regularly to cook all over. They are ready when the skin is completely charred and cracked. Repeat with the rest, then place in a colander to cool. Place them under cold running water, holding the stalk while peeling off the skin. Remove the tops with a knife and leave to drain.

Add the garlic and some salt to a mixing bowl with the aubergines and, using a pestle, break up the flesh of the aubergines, keeping some parts chunky. Add the chopped veg, herbs, half of the pomegranate seeds, the lemon juice and olive oil. Toss to combine and taste for lemon and salt. Transfer to a serving plate and garnish with the remaining pomegranate seeds and the lemon zest. Serve alongside *khobez mekli*.

Batata Mekliyeh
Hand-cut Fried Potato Chips

Hand-cut fried potato chips are iconic to every Lebanese weekend spread.

1.5kg (3lb 5oz) floury potatoes, such as
 Maris Piper
750ml (25fl oz/3 cups) neutral oil, for
 deep-frying
flaky sea salt

Wash and scrub the potatoes and cut them into discs and then into matches, not too thick or they won't cook through. Place in a bowl of water to stop them from turning brown. Heat a wok or frying pan (skillet) with the oil and, once hot, add a generous handful of potatoes, working in batches.

Once the potatoes are golden, remove with a slotted spoon and place on a plate lined with sheets of paper towel to absorb any excess oil while you cook the rest. Salt generously and serve immediately.

The day before
* Smoke the aubergines, peel and strain and place in an airtight container in the fridge overnight; ensure you strain them again 30 minutes before use
* Wash, pick and dry all the parsley for the tabbouleh, as well as the lettuce, and store in an airtight container in the fridge
* Fry the Lebanese bread and, once cooled, store in an airtight bag, somewhere cool
* Fry the nuts for the *sayadiyeh* and *samkeh harra* and store in an airtight container in the fridge once cooled
* Deseed the pomegranates and place in an airtight container in the fridge
* Make the *tarator* and store in an airtight container in the fridge
* Place the whole fish fillets between two pieces of baking parchment and lay flat in an airtight container in the fridge
* Wash the head and bones well and place in an airtight bag in the fridge
* Finely chop the onions for the rice and place them in an airtight container in the fridge
* Wash the whiting and place on baking parchment in an airtight container in the fridge

In the morning
* Prepare the remaining ingredients for the tabbouleh and the aubergine salad (both without dressing) and place in the fridge until ready to dress and serve
* Make the tahini sauce for the *samkeh harra* and set aside in the fridge until ready to bake
* Prepare the potatoes and leave to dry on some paper towel
* Place the fish carcass in the oven to roast
* Fry the fish fillets for the rice, then set aside
* Fry the onions
* Remove the tray of fish carcass, add the onions and place over a high heat on the stove
* Add the onion stock to the rice to cook.
* Sear the large fillets and bake the *samkeh harra*
* Begin frying the hand-cut chips in batches while you prepare the rest of the spread
* Assemble the smoky aubergine salad and serve
* Begin frying the whiting and place the *tarator* in a bowl
* Mix the tabbouleh and assemble ready to serve
* Assemble the rice on a platter with fried fish and nuts
* Garnish the s*amkeh harra* and serve
* Plate and serve the chips
* Plate and serve the whiting

Min Edain Emi

From Our Mothers' Hands

A collection of Lebanese spreads wouldn't be complete without a tribute to Mahshi Warak Enab, stuffed vine leaves (page 112). This iconic dish is eaten all over the Levant and is popular in Lebanon due to the abundance of vines across the region. Once the summer season is over, the leaves are preserved to ensure this dish can be enjoyed throughout the year, a cherished part of all festive spreads and celebrations.

As the end of spring draws near, with longer days and balmy evenings, I find myself running to the side of my house where my father-in-law planted a cutting from his grape vine, anticipating when the first few leaves will appear. Their arrival brings a sense of joy and celebration that summer is here and long outdoor lunches will soon be enjoyed again.

Aarishe (pronounced ah-ree-she) is the Arabic word for grapevine and grammatically it is a feminine noun. My *tayta* would always say the *aarishe* was full of *barake*, or blessings and goodness, for not only can she be replanted and reproduced from a small cutting, with each leaf you take, a younger, healthier leaf will grow back in its place. During her season, she requires very little to nurture her, as she protects, offering an abundance of leaves to nourish both the young and old who have gathered around the table.

According to my mother, the most important ingredients when preparing vine leaves are patience and care; it is a mindfulness operation that happens in stages, bringing together many hands. The first stage is my favourite: harvesting the leaves, discarding the overly coarse ones that have had too much sun and sorting the rest into piles by size. The first leaves that appear are the softest and are best saved to use to scoop up tabbouleh. The smaller leaves are used for Mahshi Warak Enab (page 112) and the larger leaves reserved for Warak Enab bi Zeit (page 140) or vine leaves cooked in oil, a vegetarian mezza side dish.

The most arduous stage is the stuffing and rolling of the vine leaves, and one my *tayta* would use as an opportunity to invite her neighbours to come over and help – a great opportunity to bond. The endless hours spent rolling vine leaves with my mother was how I learnt so much about my grandmother and the courage of her decision to leave her home and community once the war broke out.

Eating Mahshi Warak Enab for Sunday lunch at the end of the week served as a reminder that all was well in the world. Mum would nominate the closest male to the kitchen to flip the tall pot, revealing a mountain of steam, like a round of applause for our blessed mothers, and beneath it meticulously rolled vine leaves resting under succulent cuts of lamb falling off the bone.

Left and below preparing *mahshi warak enab*

One story replays in my mind that sums up the magnitude of this remarkable dish.

My friend Ali's mother, Hesen — an Arabic name that means magnificent and radiant — was an outstanding cook. She gathered her extended family for dinner every Tuesday. These dinners, just like Sunday lunch, were sacred.

When Hesen became terminally ill, her only fear was becoming dependant. After her surgery, she began her rehabilitation journey. Rolling vine leaves helped with her fine motor skills and was an activity she enjoyed. For months, without the knowledge of her family, she rolled a small pile of vine leaves each day and had her husband place them in the freezer.

After her passing, Ali's father surprised his family with the accumulated piles of rolled vine leaves that Hesen had secretly prepared for her funeral. One last time, hundreds of people would gather in a community hall to savour the last meal Hesen would ever prepare for them, a large pot of *mahshi warak enab*.

Mahshi Warak Enab
Stuffed Vine Leaves

If you have access to fresh grape vine leaves, start by removing the stalks carefully. Wash them with cold water, then blanch them in a pot of boiling water for a few minutes, until they turn a khaki colour. Once softened, rinse under cold water and strain. Squeeze any excess water before rolling. For large leaves, cut them in the centre, turn one of the halves towards you, add the stuffing in the middle, fold it over twice before tucking the edges in and roll tightly. Any leftover fresh leaves can be frozen in an airtight bag for up to a year. Leave to thaw and refresh by blanching in a pot of boiling water. I like to prepare the stuffed vine leaves in stages and freeze them before the day I plan to cook them. This can be done up to a month before.

If you are using preserved leaves bought from a Middle Eastern or Mediterranean grocer, drain and boil them as above for about 6 minutes to soften the leaves and remove any excess salt from the brine.

750g (1lb 10oz) fresh or preserved
   vine leaves
2 whole lamb necks; ask the butcher
   to cut them into thirds
2 lamb shanks; ask the butcher to cut
   them into thirds
4 bay leaves
1 stick of cinnamon
1 tbsp Sabaa Bharat (page 20)
juice of 5–6 lemons

For the stuffing
500g (1lb 2oz) coarse minced
   (ground) lamb
720g (1lb 9½oz/4 cups) medium-grain rice
sea salt, to taste
1 tsp Sabaa Bharat (page 20)

To prevent breakage when cooking, you need to be able to roll the leaf twice before tucking the sides in; this keeps the leaves and rice intact. Most importantly, the stuffed leaves need to be weighed down to avoid them floating.

To make the stuffing, combine the mince, rice, salt and *bharat* in a mixing bowl, using your hands to ensure the meat and rice mixture are well combined and seasoned. Taste a little on the tip of your tongue – it should not be bland.

At a table or kitchen bench, have all the ingredients within arm's reach. Spread out the vine leaves on a plate or tray, put the stuffing in a bowl and have ready a clean chopping board to hold each leaf down while you stuff it so it doesn't slide around. I also keep a small knife beside me to trim any stems that are still attached, and a container or tray for the stuffed leaves.

Lay a leaf flat, vein-side up and the base of the leaf (longest side) nearest to you. Place 1 teaspoon of stuffing 1cm (½in) away from the base, spread it across the width and begin to roll it over twice before tucking in the sides and rolling it up to close. It should resemble a very small cigar. Be mindful not to overstuff the leaves or put too much pressure when you are rolling, as the rice needs room to expand once cooked. Each roll should be about 1cm (½in) in diameter and 6cm (2½in) long. Repeat with the rest of the vine leaves and stuffing.

When you cook the leaves, it is crucial you have a large enough pot, one that will comfortably fit the meat at the bottom, several rows of stacked vine leaves, a plate and a weight and then finally the lid.

Put the lamb cuts in a pot and fill with water until covered. Add the bay leaves and cinnamon. Bring the pot to a boil and skim off any scum that rises. Continue to boil for 5 minutes. Tip the lamb cuts into a colander in the sink and rinse well under cold water before placing them in a larger, heavy-based pan that you will be cooking the vine leaves in; I like to use cast aluminium. Arrange the lamb cuts around the base, stacking them if there are too many, and season them generously with salt and the *bharat*. I like to place the bay leaves and cinnamon on top of the lamb. Begin to layer the vine leaves on top of the meat, all around the pot evenly, layer upon layer, neatly and tightly packed until they all fit in the pan.

Place the pot on a high heat and add 1.4 litres (50fl oz/6 cups) of water along with a plate and a weight on top of the plate so the leaves don't move around while cooking. Bring to the boil, cover and continue to cook over a high heat for 20 minutes, reduce to a medium-low heat and cook for at least 6 hours. I like to slow-cook this for up to 12 hours, if I have the time. While the pot is cooking, you must keep an eye on the water level as it will require a top up during the process. A good way to determine if there is enough water is if you tip the pot slightly to the left or right the broth should flow easily to the side. If not, add 250ml (8½fl oz/1 cup) of water.

An hour before the end of the cooking time, squeeze the lemon juice all around the pot, holding the sides of the pot to evenly distribute. Put the lid back on and put the pot on a high heat to bring it to a boil. After 30 minutes, remove the lid, the weight and plate and let the leaves simmer on low for a further 30 minutes. Taste to check the lemon and salt.

If you feel there is too much liquid in the pot, you can pour it out into a bowl, before flipping the pot, to ladle over your plate, I personally love to drink it.

To serve, place a large tray with raised edges on top of the open pot and carefully tip the pot upside down, holding the dish in place, then lifting the pot to reveal the succulent lamb, tender vine leaves and rich broth.

I like to serve this with a platter of mint, spring onion (scallions), radish and fresh garlic, and eat with plenty of Lebanese bread, dipping the vine leaves into the cold Laban w' Khyar (page 117).

There are many memories that come with preparing and feasting on *mahshi warak enab* (stuffed vine leaves). Plan to do the stuffing and rolling with company; it turns a laborious task into a therapeutic activity.

Below serving *mahshi warak enab*
Right *salatet loz akhdar w' aashab*

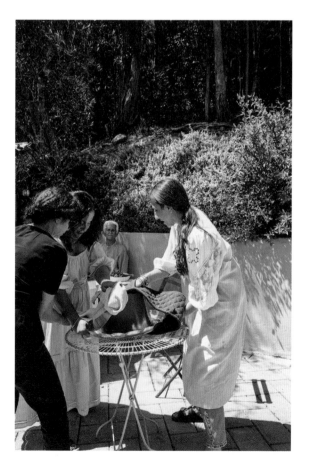

Kibbeh Nayyeh
Ground Raw Meat with Fine Bulgur Wheat and Spices

To me, this dish tells a story of each region in Lebanon, the environment and its people. Here, the hero is the flavour and texture of the freshly ground meat, which has subtle hints of *bharat*, basil and freshly grated nutmeg.

Traditionally, *kibbeh nayyeh* was made in a *jerin* and *muddaqa* (large stone pestle and mortar), its preparation a test of patience and stamina. This ancient vessel is still used today in Lebanon's rural villages to pound the fresh cuts of lamb as well as the bulgur wheat, onion and spices. In most homes, modern appliances have replaced the pestle and mortar, the result still delicious and undeniably easier.

The lamb should be young, and a deep pinky-red colour, lean and velvety in texture. The meat must be trimmed of all fat and gristle before preparation. In cities with large Lebanese communities, it is possible to find a butcher who specializes in providing ready-ground *kibbeh* meat. This is not regular minced (ground) meat. It is like a lean paste and so fresh it can be eaten raw. Let your butcher know you are cooking *kibbeh nayyeh* or ask for *kibbeh* mince. If you cannot buy the meat, substitute the dish with Tomato Kibbeh (page 147).

170g (6oz/1 cup) fine bulgur wheat
1 small brown onion
3 stems of fresh basil
sea salt, to taste
½ tsp freshly ground black pepper
1 tsp Sabaa Bharat (page 20)
½ tsp freshly grated nutmeg
1 small fresh red chilli (optional), sliced
500g (1lb 2oz) minced (ground) *kibbeh* meat (a combination of beef and lamb, see recipe introduction)
a platter of fresh mint, spring onions (scallions) and radishes, to serve
extra virgin olive oil or chilli walnut oil (see page 118), as needed

Begin by washing the bulgur, then strain in a sieve and squeeze any excess water out with your hands.

Finely chop the onion and place it in a pestle and mortar along with the basil leaves, salt, spices and chilli (if using) and pound into a smooth paste. Alternatively, you can use a small food processor to do this but do make sure the onion is very finely processed.

In a mixing bowl wide enough to fit your arms, add the meat, bulgur and onion mixture, and have a small bowl of water handy beside you. Dip your hands in the water and begin kneading the mixture, wetting your hands occasionally if the mixture gets too sticky, until it is all combined. Water is not an ingredient, so use it sparingly.

Once combined, place the *kibbeh* in the centre of a large platter and, using your hands, mould it into an oval shape. Using the handle of a spoon, create a pattern across the *kibbeh*, by pressing it into the meat. Serve with fresh mint, spring onions and crunchy radishes and plenty of extra virgin olive oil, or a drizzle of the chilli walnut oil (see page 118) if you prefer. I like to serve this with fresh Lebanese bread.

Laban w' Khyar
Garlic Yogurt with Cucumber and Mint

A bowl of cold *laban w' khyar* is perfect alongside the lemony *warak enab* but its uses are endless.

2 garlic cloves, crushed
500ml (17fl oz/2 cups) thick Greek yogurt
2 Lebanese cucumbers, finely diced
2 sprigs of mint, finely chopped, plus a few
  leaves to garnish
1 tbsp dried mint, plus extra to garnish
sea salt, to taste

Place the garlic and a pinch of salt in a pestle and mortar and crush well to form a paste. Put the garlic paste in a mixing bowl with the yogurt, cucumbers, fresh and dried mint and combine to form a thick paste. Add 250ml (8½fl oz/1 cup) of water and mix well to loosen up the consistency. Place in the fridge until ready to serve garnished with a sprinkling of dried mint and a few fresh leaves.

Salatet Loz Akhdar bil Aashab
Green Almond and Herb Salad

My father-in-law has a wonderful green thumb and whenever I pass by his place he usually fills up a bag of whatever fresh herbs and greens he has growing in abundance: *bakleh* (purslane), za'atar (wild thyme), oregano, mint, parsley, watercress and *jarjeer* (rocket/arugula). No matter the selection, this tart, bitter and peppery salad always has a place at the table, and here it is perfect with the *kibbeh nayyeh* and *warak enab*, stuffed between fresh Lebanese bread.

½ bunch of mint
1 bunch of purslane (*bakleh*)
½ bunch of oregano
½ bunch of parsley
1 bunch of rocket (arugula)
1 Spanish onion, finely chopped
250g (9oz) young green almonds
juice of ½ lemon
extra virgin olive oil
sea salt, to taste
1 tsp sumac

Wash the fresh herbs well, ensuring all dirt has been removed, then leave to dry completely. Pick the leaves of the mint, purslane, oregano and parsley. Chop the mint leaves and rocket into 1cm (½in) lengths and add to a bowl with the herbs. Wash and thinly slice the almonds and add. Dress the salad with the lemon juice, extra virgin olive oil, salt and sumac and gently toss with your hands. Serve immediately.

Zeit w' Har
Chilli Walnut Oil

This textured oil has a strong kick and is the perfect contrast to the *kibbeh*.

100g (3½oz/1 cup) walnuts
1 tsp paprika
1 tsp chilli powder
250ml (8½fl oz/1 cup) extra virgin olive oil
1 tbsp lemon zest
sea salt, to taste

Roast the walnuts in a hot oven until lightly toasted, or shake in a dry frying pan (skillet), then tip out onto a plate and leave to cool. Chop roughly with a sharp kitchen knife. Place all the ingredients into a bowl and adjust the salt to taste.

This mixture keeps well in a jar in the fridge and can be eaten drizzled on just about anything.

Up to one month before
* Stuff and roll the vine leaves, then freeze

The day before
* Either remove from the freezer or begin stuffing and rolling the vine leaves, then place in a container in the fridge

In the morning (at least 6 hours before)
* Prepare the meat and add to the pot
* Add the vine leaves to the pan and begin the cooking
* Prepare the onion mixture and bulgur wheat for the *kibbeh* and set aside in the fridge
* Prepare the *laban w' khyar* and set aside in the fridge
* Wash the herbs for the salad, leave to dry, then set aside in the fridge
* Continuously check on the vine leaves and their water level, adding boiling water if you need to top up
* Squeeze the lemons and set aside
* Wash and trim the vegetables and herbs for the platter, then set aside in the fridge until ready to serve

One hour before serving
* Add the lemon juice to the vine leaves
* Combine the onion and bulgur wheat with the *kibbeh* meat, plate the *kibbeh*, then set aside in the fridge until ready to serve
* Dress and plate the salad
* Plate the *laban w' khyar* and serve
* Serve the vine leaves

Moujtamaa

Community

On a particular visit to the Lebanese grocers, there is a high bustling energy, an organized chaos and yet a sense of calm. As usual, the walls are stacked floor to ceiling with different brands of tahini, chickpeas and fava beans and bags filled with various sizes of bulgur wheat. The fridges are replenished daily with cows' yogurt, goats' yogurt, milk and cheeses, both fermented and dried. The herbs and vegetables are seasonal and abundant. Large bunches of parsley and mint for endless bowls of tabbouleh sit alongside bright pink radishes and spring onions.

Mum always shops and cooks seasonally, picking through the unruly bunches of endive and chicory, always selecting the smaller grey zucchini and okra when she finds them. I smile at the older man unpacking the vegetables, tossing the damaged ones into a cardboard box under the trolley, smiling, his mind elsewhere. He recognizes me, for I am here every week and calls me *amo*, a term of endearment, as if he is my uncle. 'Allah ya tik al afyeh' (God grant you health, usually said when someone is working hard), I start our conversation, and he asks me if I need anything. His warmth and charm are embedded in the walls of the shop, and I wonder if he knows how much I look forward to our often weekly interactions.

The queue is long, but miraculously moves swiftly. As I stand in line I watch as the locals greet one another, conversing in Arabic, picking up where they left off several weeks ago at the same place, a productive meeting point. Their names and faces are different but their narratives are similar, with cooking often a central part of their lives.

Over the years the faces at the grocers and butchers become more and more familiar and the verbal exchanges become personal banter, conversations between customer and shop owner both dependent on one another to survive. Before this community of 'Little Lebanon' was built, older generations had to drive all over to find ingredients. Trips to the grocer would be like a treasure hunt. Every few months a new ingredient would materialize and *tayta* would call the aunties or neighbours, telling them to come and take their share of what she had bought.

The time I spent at the grocers, bakeries and butchers helped shape my understanding of the Lebanese living in the diaspora and I marvelled at how they continued to expand and grow as an organic ecosystem feeding off itself and flourishing. Migration meant sacrificing many things – their sunlit apartment in Tripoli, their butchers and souks, their neighbours and friends – but some things, over time, could be recreated. Preparing food for loved ones and those precious moments shared around the table gave mealtimes so much meaning, no matter how far they were from home.

Left and below *shish barak*

My *tayta*'s *shish barak* were shaped into half moons, 'like your dad's ears', she would tease my Mum, who spent years with her in the kitchen.

Shish Barak
Meat-filled Dumplings with a Rich Garlic
Yogurt Sauce

We would spend lazy afternoons
preparing these meat dumplings. They are
quite fiddly, but they freeze well. During
the week, Mum would poach them in
garlic yogurt broth, but at the weekend
they were transformed into a textured
main dish layered with so much flavour.
The dumplings are fried until golden,
giving them a deliciously crunchy exterior,
and served with the yogurt ladled on top
and a shower of ghee-fried pine nuts.

Makes about 100 small *shish barak*,
enough for 2–3 meals

For the dough
500g (1lb 2oz/4 cups) plain
   (all-purpose) flour
1 tsp salt
1 tsp sugar
125ml (4fl oz/½ cup) olive oil
neutral oil, for frying

For the meat
800g (1lb 12oz) coarsely minced
   (ground) lamb (or a combination
   of beef and lamb)
4 medium-sized brown onions, finely diced
1 tbsp Sabaa Bharat (page 20)
1 tbsp salt
1 tbsp ghee

For the yogurt broth
1 litre (34fl oz/4 cups) goats' yogurt
   (or set yogurt)
1 tbsp cornflour (cornstarch)
4 large garlic cloves, crushed
2 tbsp ghee
1 bunch of coriander (cilantro), stalks and
   leaves finely chopped
sea salt, to taste

To garnish
75g (2½oz/½ cup) pine nuts
¼ tsp chilli powder or smoked paprika
   (optional)

For the dough, sift the flour into a bowl,
add the salt and sugar and mix to
incorporate. Place the olive oil in a jug
with 500ml (17fl oz/2 cups) of water,
then gradually add it to the flour, using
a wooden spoon to combine. Using your
hands, begin to knead the mixture and
bring it together into a smooth dough,
then cover and leave to rest for 1 hour.

In the meantime, heat a frying pan (skillet)
and add the meat and onions, then mix
well. Add the *bharat* and salt. Once the
meat liquid has evaporated, add the ghee
and mix well, then set aside to cool.

Cut the rested dough into 4 equal parts
and begin working with one piece, keeping
the others covered. Roll it out thinly, about
1–2mm thick, and cut out circles using a
7cm (3in) cookie cutter or the rim of a
glass. Place 1 teaspoon of the filling in the
middle and fold over the edges to make
a half moon. Seal the edges, then take
both corners of the crescent and pinch
them together – see page 124. If you are
eating these on the day or the following
day, place them in the fridge until you are
ready to cook. Or, you can freeze them,
making sure they are separated and
frozen individually on a tray before you
place them together in a freezer bag.

To make the yogurt broth, place a heavy-
based saucepan on a high heat, add the
yogurt and 200ml (7fl oz/scant 1 cup)
water and begin stirring. Dissolve the
cornflour in 120ml (4fl oz/½ cup) of water,
add to the pan and stir continuously until
you reach boiling point, then reduce to
medium. Make sure it is slightly bubbling
and cook for 30 minutes, uncovered.

Mix the garlic with some salt. Add
a heaped tablespoon of the ghee to a
frying pan (skillet) on a medium heat,
add the garlic and coriander, then remove
from the heat as soon as the ghee
melts and the ingredients have married.
Add this garlic mixture to the bubbling
yogurt broth.

To cook the *shish barak*, fill a wok or frying pan (skillet) with enough neutral oil to just cover the top of the dumplings. Once the oil is hot, place a few dumplings in the pan and fry for a few minutes until golden. Once fried, scoop out and place on a plate covered with paper towels to absorb any excess oil while you fry the remainder.

To serve, heat a small frying pan with the remaining tablespoon of ghee and fry the pine nuts until golden, being careful not to burn them. Place the fried *shish barak* in a deep, flat serving dish and ladle the yogurt broth over the top until they are submerged halfway in the yogurt. Scatter the ghee and pine nuts all over, and watch as they crackle and sizzle. Serve immediately, sprinkled with chilli powder or smoked paprika, if you like.

Mujaddara
Spiced Lentil Rice with
Caramelized Onions

Mujaddara is a humble, comforting dish calling for the most basic of pantry ingredients. Its versatility makes it the champion of many week-night dishes and spreads. The combination of the *mujaddara* and *shish barak* is spectacular in this spread, the lentil rice making the perfect base to soak up all the flavours from the garlic yogurt broth.

2 large brown onions, thinly sliced
250g (9oz/1½ cups) green lentils
350g (12oz/2 cups) long-grain rice
1 tsp cumin
1 tsp Sabaa Bharat (page 20)
1 heaped tbsp ghee
60ml (2fl oz/¼ cup) olive oil
sea salt, to taste

Season the onions with salt, then set aside.

Wash the lentils well and place in a medium-sized non-stick saucepan along with 1 litre (34fl oz/4 cups) of water, cover and bring to the boil. Wash the rice well and, once the lentils are half cooked, add the rice, spices and salt, then mix and bring to a boil before turning down the heat to low and leaving to simmer for 20 minutes.

Place the onions, ghee and oil in a medium-sized frying pan (skillet) on a high heat and cook until the onions have turned a dark brown colour; stir constantly. Drain the oil into the rice pan and set aside the caramelized onions.

To serve, place the *mujaddara* on a deep, flat serving dish and mount it so it has some height. Garnish with the caramelized onions.

Mum always served her *shish barak* just as her mother would, alongside a mountain of *mujaddara* (lentil rice) and a freshly shaved cabbage salad with plates of *bemyeh* and *hindbeh* (endive/chicory).

Below *mujaddara*
Right *salatet hindbeh*

Salatet Malfouf
Cabbage Salad

Salatet malfouf is synonymous with *mujaddara* – they are a perfect pair.

½ round white cabbage
1 large Spanish onion, sliced into wedges
1 punnet of cherry tomatoes, quartered
½ bunch of mint, leaves only, sliced
   into strips
1 bunch of fresh oregano, leaves only,
   plus extra to garnish
1 garlic clove, crushed
120ml (4fl oz/½ cup) extra virgin olive oil
120ml (4fl oz/5½ cups) lemon juice
sea salt, to taste

Discard any damaged outer leaves and slice the cabbage as thinly as possible, then place it in a mixing bowl. Add the onion, cherry tomatoes, mint and oregano and mix together. Make the dressing by crushing the garlic with salt and putting it in a small bowl with the extra virgin olive oil and lemon juice. Mix well. Dress the salad, garnish with the extra oregano and serve immediately in a deep, flat bowl.

Ma'anek
Lebanese Sausages in
Pomegranate Molasses

Lebanese sausages are quite small, usually the size of your thumb, and are filled with fatty minced (ground) lamb, garlic, chilli and pine nuts. If you can't find the real thing, use any small good-quality sausages.

1kg (2lb 4oz) *ma'anek*
neutral oil, for frying

For the dressing
3 garlic cloves, crushed
2 tbsp extra virgin olive oil
4 tbsp pomegranate molasses
juice of 1 lemon
sea salt, to taste

For the garnish
1 tbsp ghee
75g (2½oz/½ cup) pine nuts
a handful of parsley, roughly chopped
½ pomegranate, deseeded (page 31)
fresh Lebanese bread, to serve

For the dressing, combine all the ingredients in a bowl and set aside.

Separate the sausages and use a fork to pierce them a few times all over. Add some neutral oil to a frying pan (skillet), enough to just submerge the sausages, and when the oil is hot, add the sausages to the pan without overcrowding. Once they are browned and cooked through, about 10 minutes, place them straight into a flat serving dish and keep warm while you cook the remainder.

In a frying pan (skillet), heat the ghee and fry the pine nuts until golden brown.

Assemble the sausages on a serving plate. Drizzle the dressing all over, garnish with the parsley, pomegranate seeds and pine nuts, and serve with fresh Lebanese bread.

Salatet Hindbeh
Warm Wild Green Salad

Of the two ways we traditionally prepare *hindbeh*, this is certainly my favourite. It is such a versatile mezza dish that can be served warm or cold.

1 large bunch of wild chicory, endive or
   dandelion leaves
sea salt, to taste
3 garlic cloves, crushed
juice and zest of 1 lemon, plus 1 lemon cut
   into wedges
60ml (2fl oz/¼ cup) extra virgin olive oil
1 tsp Aleppo pepper, to serve
fresh Lebanese bread (optional), to serve

Chop the chicory into 3cm (¼in) lengths and soak in the sink with plenty of coarse salt. I usually change the water 2–3 times until it runs clear. Put the chicory in a large saucepan and cover with boiling water, add a pinch of salt and place over a high heat. Once boiling, cook for about 10 minutes, before tipping into a colander. Run under cold water to cool it down and leave to drain.

Meanwhile, prepare the dressing by crushing the garlic with salt and mixing it in a bowl with the lemon juice and oil.

Once the greens have cooled slightly, press them between your hands to squeeze out any excess water and place them in a mixing bowl. Separate the wilted leaves slightly, toss the dressing through, garnish with lemon zest and serve with a drizzle of extra virgin olive oil, lemon wedges, Aleppo pepper and fresh Lebanese bread.

Bemyeh bil Zeit
Okra Tossed with Tomato and Oil

Smaller okra are ideal for this as they are only lightly sautéed and don't require much cooking; the larger ones remain tough and are often quite stringy inside. Many Mediterranean grocers sell bags of frozen okra, which also work fine, but if you happen to come across the small, fresh ones, don't hesitate to buy them.

750g (1lb 10oz) okra (ladies' fingers)
180ml (6fl oz/¾ cup) olive oil
1 large onion, thinly sliced
5 garlic cloves, sliced
1 punnet of cherry tomatoes, sliced in half
¼ tsp paprika
¼ tsp ground black pepper
a handful of coriander (cilantro) leaves
a pinch of Aleppo pepper
sea salt, to taste

If using fresh okra, wash well, drain and remove the tops by cutting around the tip so each is pointed and not flat, then set aside. If you are using frozen okra, defrost completely and pat dry before cooking.

Heat a wok or large frying pan (skillet), add the oil and fry half the okra to give them a crispy exterior, then set aside on a plate lined with paper towels. Repeat with the other half. Return the okra to the oil, add the onion, garlic and cherry tomatoes and toss. Season with paprika, salt and pepper, then transfer to a serving dish. Garnish with coriander and a pinch of Aleppo pepper.

Below *salatet malfouf*
Right *ma'anek*

Make beforehand
* *Shish barak* can be made and frozen for up to 3 months beforehand if you use fresh meat in the filling

The day before
* Wash and cook the *hindbeh*, squeeze out the water and place in an airtight container in the fridge
* Wash the okra, remove the tips and leave to dry before placing in an airtight container in the fridge
* Wash all the cabbage salad ingredients and leave to dry before placing in an airtight container in the fridge
* Chop the cabbage and place in an airtight container in the fridge
* Make the salad dressing and set aside in the fridge
* Deseed the half a pomegranate and place in an airtight container in the fridge
* Wash all the green herbs used for garnish, leave to dry, then set aside in the fridge in an airtight container
* Make the dressing for the *ma'anek*; set aside in the fridge

On the day
* Salt the onions for the *mujaddara*, then set aside
* Make the *mujaddara* and cover to keep it warm
* Fry the onions, then set aside to garnish
* Make the yogurt broth for the *shish barak*, then set aside in the pot; if it cools slightly you can reheat it before serving
* Remove the *hindbeh* from the fridge, make the dressing and toss before serving
* Fry the *shish barak* and set aside in a serving dish
* Make the *bemyeh bil zeit* and serve.
* Fry the *ma'anek* and place on the serving dish without the dressing or garnish

To serve
* Place the *mujaddara* in a serving dish and garnish with the caramelized onions
* Place the yogurt broth on the heat
* Toss the *salata malfouf* with the dressing and place on a serving dish
* Fry the pine nuts for the *ma'anek*, add the dressing, garnish and serve
* Remove the yogurt from the heat and fry the pine nuts for the *shish barak* in the ghee
* Ladle the yogurt broth over the *shish barak*, garnish with the hot pine nuts and serve immediately

Sayran Nabaty

Vegetarian Picnic

The Lebanese diet is broadly vegetarian, although Lebanese emigrants tend to eat more meat because of its availability. Meat is generally reserved for weekend gatherings, religious celebrations and special occasions, and even then would make up one or two dishes as part of a spread. Vegetarian dishes tell a story of Lebanon's rich, fertile land and the seasons that bring in the plentiful crops. Whereas meat dishes tend to be similar across the country, the vegetarian dishes celebrate the differences between the regions in terms of agriculture, trade and culinary influences.

As Lebanese people we love to picnic, in parks or by the sea. As a social worker within the Arab community, Mum had an eclectic circle of friends and colleagues who had a remarkable influence on her cooking, particularly when it came to vegetarian dishes. I vividly remember the large picnics at the weekend where everyone would bring a plate of something to share, each dish traditional and from a different corner of Lebanon.

Vegetarian mezza dishes are traditionally eaten at room temperature and, with no heating or refrigeration required, are ideal for delicious outdoor spreads. This way of eating continues at home, the dishes changing with the seasons, hearty fresh mezza dishes that are both filling and perfect for entertaining. We also make Mujaddara (page 127) and Loubiyeh Arida (page 165), but Mum's speciality has always been Warak Enab bi Zeit (page 140).

Growing up, I remember listening to the banter from Mum and her friends, every weekend debating each dish with its signature flavours or ingredients – all cooked with love and nurture in mind. This spread is an ode to the weekend picnics that united the Lebanese migrants who fled a war that aimed to separate them, but, in fact, only made their love of food and one another stronger.

Warak Enab bi Zeit
Stuffed Grapevine Leaves

The anticipation is always high at the beginning of the grape vine season and sourcing fresh leaves to make this dish becomes the first mission to accomplish. When harvesting and preserving, the larger leaves are used for this dish and the much smaller leaves are reserved for Mahshi Warak Enab (page 112).

750ml (25fl oz/3-cup) jar of vine leaves in brine or 500g (1lb 2oz) fresh vine leaves
2 medium-sized white potatoes, sliced
2 medium-sized tomatoes, sliced

For the filling
1 large bunch of flat-leaf parsley, finely chopped
½ bunch of mint leaves, finely chopped
4 medium-sized tomatoes, finely chopped
1 bunch of spring onions (scallions), finely sliced
1 small brown onion, finely chopped
juice of 2 lemons
1 heaped tbsp tomato purée (paste)
2 tbsp pomegranate molasses
sea salt, to taste
1 tsp Sabaa Bharat (page 20)
½ tsp chilli powder (optional but recommended)
1 tsp sumac
120ml (4fl oz/½ cup) extra virgin olive oil
350g (12oz/2 cups) medium-grain rice, washed well

For the cooking liquid
1 litre (34fl oz/4 cups) water
120ml (4fl oz/½ cup) olive oil
juice of 1 lemon
2 tbsp good-quality tomato purée (paste)
2 tbsp pomegranate molasses
¼ tsp Sabaa Bharat (page 20)
¼ tsp chilli powder (optional)
sea salt

To garnish
lemon wedges

Prepare the fresh vine leaves as outlined on page 112.

If you are using vine leaves in brine, boil them in water for 5 minutes. Drain and let cool, then squeeze out any excess water.

There is no magic number for how many stuffed vine leaves per quantity of filling, just always make sure you have extra leaves to account for all the filling. Any extra leaves can be frozen in an airtight bag for later use.

For the filling, prepare the parsley, mint, tomatoes and spring onions as you would a tabbouleh (page 98) and place in a large bowl. Add the remaining filling ingredients, leaving the rice until last, and toss well to combine. Taste for seasoning.

On a clean, flat surface place a leaf shiny-side down and veiny-side up and add a heaped teaspoon of the filling 1cm (½in) from the base, where the stem was. Fold the bottom edge up to cover the filling and roll twice before bringing the sides in. Continue to roll until you have enclosed the filling with the leaf. Repeat with the rest.

Drizzle some olive oil in a large, heavy-based saucepan, and line with unrolled vine leaves and then the potatoes; these serve to protect the stuffed vine leaves from burning or getting stuck to the bottom of the pan. Lay a few of the tomatoes on top of the potatoes and reserve a few to scatter throughout the vine leaves in the pan. Begin to assemble the stuffed vine leaves. The stuffed leaves should face into the centre of the pan. Work your way around the base in a circle and ensure they are packed in tightly so they don't open up when cooking.

Mix all the ingredients for the cooking liquid in a bowl, ensuring every ingredient is dissolved before you pour it over the vine leaves. Place a plate face down to cover the vine leaves, bring to a boil and then simmer on a medium-low heat for up to 3 hours, or until the stuffed leaves are cooked – to check, taste the top one. Once cooked, leave to rest in the pan for 10 minutes to set before you flip the pan. When you are ready to serve, place a large serving plate or tray over the pan, put your hand on the top of the tray covering the pan and the other hand underneath the bottom of the pan. Make sure you have a grip on the pan. Flip it inwards towards you and gently lift the pan, keeping in mind the liquid, although there is not usually much.

Garnish with freshly sliced lemon wedges and serve warm or at room temperature.

Hindbeh bil Zeit
Wild Greens

In Arabic we use the word *hindbeh* to describe wild endive, chicory and dandelion – all three work well in this dish depending on what is in season and what you have access to. The flavours are quite similar, though the curly endive cooks much quicker and requires only half of the cooking time.

1kg (2lb 4oz) curly endive or chicory
  or dandelion
80ml (3fl oz/⅓ cup) neutral oil
4 large onions, thinly sliced
100ml (3½fl oz/scant ½ cup) olive oil
3 garlic cloves, thinly sliced
sea salt
1 lemon, to serve
Lebanese bread, to serve

Prepare the endive as described on page 131.

Heat the neutral oil on medium–high in a medium-sized sauté pan and add half of the onions. Allow them to crisp up to a very deep caramel, stirring occasionally so as not to burn. Remove from the heat and strain off any excess oil.

Place a large pan or wok over a medium heat, add the olive oil, the remaining onions and the garlic and cook until soft and fragrant. Add the greens and salt and toss to combine with the onion and garlic.

To serve, place the cooked greens on a serving dish, garnish with the crispy onions and serve with wedges of lemon and fresh Lebanese bread.

Left and below *warak enab bi zeit*
Below *hindbeh bil zeit*

Muhammara
Roasted Pepper and Walnut Dip

The first time I tried this dish was at a Palestinian friend's place, who had her *man'al* (charcoal barbecue) lined with bright red peppers. Her Syrian mother-in-law shared the recipe with her, as the origins of the dish lie in the city of Aleppo in Syria. When I begged them both for the recipe they listed the ingredients with no quantities, explained a few of the steps with exaggerated hand gestures and assured me of the forgiving nature of the recipe. It has been a treasured dip for our family ever since.

1.5kg (3lb 5oz) red (bell) peppers
100ml (3½fl oz/scant ½ cup) olive oil, plus extra for frying
200g (7oz/2 cups) walnuts
1 large Spanish onion, finely chopped
5 garlic cloves, crushed
1 heaped tbsp good-quality tomato purée (paste)
2 tsp ground cumin
2 tsp Aleppo chilli
40g (1½oz/scant 1 cup) breadcrumbs
2 tbsp pomegranate molasses
1 tbsp lemon juice
sea salt, to taste

To garnish
a drizzle of extra virgin olive oil
a handful of pomegranate seeds

Preheat the oven to 200°C/400°F (gas 7). Halve the peppers, place on a baking tray lined with baking parchment and toss lightly with olive oil. Roast for about 30 minutes, or until completely softened and the skins are charred and completely black. Alternatively, you can place them on a barbecue to char.

Transfer to a bowl, cover with a dish towel and leave to cool for about 30 minutes. Once the peppers have cooled, remove the skins, stems and seeds and set aside the flesh.

Turn the oven down to 160°C/325°F (gas 4) and spread the walnuts on a baking tray lined with a clean sheet of baking parchment. Roast until they are lightly toasted, about 10 minutes.

Place a medium-sized pan on a medium–high heat with 2 tablespoons of olive oil, add the onion and cook until softened and lightly browned. Add the garlic, tomato purée and spices and cook, stirring constantly, until combined and fragrant. Remove from the heat and place into a food processor along with the peppers, breadcrumbs, pomegranate molasses and lemon juice, with another 2 tablespoons of olive oil and salt to taste. Blend to form a coarse paste. Reserve a few walnuts for garnish, then add the rest to the processor. Blend until the walnuts have broken down but have not yet formed a paste.

Transfer this to a serving dish and top with a drizzle of extra virgin olive oil, the reserved walnuts and fresh pomegranate seeds.

Kammounet Banadoura
Tomato Kibbeh

An old family friend would make this for their vegetarian mother; instead of meat, she made the mixture used in Frakeh (page 72) with overly ripe tomatoes. Finish the dish with lashings of the best extra virgin olive oil you can find and, when in season, scoop up with young green leaves picked freshly off the grape vine.

For the tomato-bulgur mixture
500g (1lb 2oz) ripe tomatoes (I like to use cherry tomatoes)
250g (9oz/1½ cups) fine brown bulgur wheat
2 heaped tbsp good-quality tomato purée (paste)

For the *kammouneh*
2 tbsp kammouneh (page 20)
½ tbsp cumin
½ tbsp Sabaa Bharat (page 20)
sea salt
1 wedge of red (bell) pepper
1 sprig of mint, leaves only
1 sprig of basil, leaves only
1 sprig of marjoram, leaves only
1 small brown onion
1 spring onion (scallion)
80g (3oz/½ cup) fine brown bulgur wheat

For the salad ingredients
1 Lebanese cucumber, finely diced
1 punnet of cherry tomatoes, cut into quarters
1 Spanish onion, finely diced
1 long green chilli, finely sliced
a handful of flat-leaf parsley, finely diced
a handful of mint, finely diced
a handful of fresh oregano leaves

To serve
extra virgin olive oil
fresh vine leaves or cos lettuce leaves
Lebanese bread

Pulse the washed, ripe tomatoes in a food processor until they are finely blended and the liquid from them is released.

Put the bulgur wheat in a deep wide bowl and cover with the tomato mixture. Use your hands or a spoon to combine the tomato juice and the bulgur, making sure not to leave any bulgur uncoated. Allow to stand for 30 minutes.

Meanwhile, for the *kammouneh*, put all the ingredients in a food processor and pulse until you see the mixture combined and crumbly. The aim is to form a loose, fragrant and crumbly mixture that will be used to flavour the tomatoes.

Put the loose *kammouneh* mixture, the tomato bulgur mixture and the tomato purée in a bowl large enough to incorporate all the ingredients. Begin to combine the mixtures together, incorporating them both as much as possible. Drizzle 2 tablespoons of olive oil throughout the mixture to help bind it together slightly.

Add the cucumber, cherry tomatoes, onion, chilli and fresh herbs to the mixture and delicately toss through. This is traditionally served heaped on a plate with a generous drizzle of extra virgin olive oil, scooped up with vine leaves and eaten with fresh Lebanese bread and a platter of fresh vegetables.

Below *ejjeh*
Right serving up vegetarian mezza

Ejjeh
Courgette and Herb Fritters

I turn to this dish when I have an abundance of fresh herbs either in the garden or in my fridge that need to be used.

2 courgettes (zucchini), grated
2 bunches of parsley, finely chopped
½ bunch of mint, finely chopped
1 bunch of dill, finely chopped
1 bunch of spring onions (scallions), finely chopped (including green stems)
1 tsp Sabaa Bharat (page 20)
½ tsp paprika
sea salt, to taste
8 eggs
1 heaped tbsp plain (all-purpose) flour
neutral oil, for frying
1 quantity of Tarator (page 80) without parsley

Grate the courgettes and squeeze out as much moisture as possible, place them in a sieve to drain further and set aside. Place the herbs, spring onions, spices, salt, eggs and flour in a large mixing bowl with the courgettes and use a hand whisk to combine.

Heat a small frying pan (skillet) and add 2 tablespoons of oil. Add 1 ladleful of the mixture to the pan and wait for the base to cook and form a crust, when it should be easy to flip with a spatula and cook the other side until golden brown.

Serve warm with a bowl of *tarator*.

Moghrabieh Trabulsiyeh
Spiced Semolina Pearls and Chickpeas

The *moghrabieh* we grew up with was a version that originated in the old souks in Tripoli. It is eaten as a street food there, packed tightly into a Lebanese bread wrap with pickles and gently cooked onions. We often had it on a platter as part of a spread, particularly during Ramadan, the aromas of the cinnamon and ghee ever so comforting. You'll find *moghrabieh* pearls in most Middle Eastern grocers and delis. If you want to use canned chickpeas, drain and rinse them, then add with the pearls.

170g (6oz/1 cup) dried chickpeas (garbanzos)
1 tsp bicarbonate of soda (baking soda)
500g (1lb 2oz) *moghrabieh* pearls
6 small brown pickling onions or 3 medium-sized onions
2 heaped tbsp ghee
1 tbsp ground cinnamon
sea salt, to taste

Prepare the chickpeas and bicarbonate of soda as described on page 22, then set aside.

Bring a saucepan of water to the boil and add the *moghrabieh* pearls, cooking them as you would pasta. Remove when they are soft and chewy, strain and set aside. Remove the skins of the onions, keeping them whole and keeping the head and roots intact so the onion doesn't fall apart. Place them in a pan of boiling water and boil for a few minutes to soften slightly. Once slightly cooled, cut the onions in half and trim the tops.

In a wok or large frying pan (skillet), heat the ghee, add the onions and toss gently to give them some colour. Add the *moghrabieh* pearls and the chickpeas along with the cinnamon and salt and toss for several minutes, or until all the flavours are combined. Serve warm with a platter of pickles.

Salatet al Shoumar
Fennel Salad

This salad is simplicity at its best. If you
don't have fresh oregano, parsley and
mint will also work, although the spice of
the oregano really is the hero here.

2 bulbs of fennel
½ pomegranate, deseeded (page 31)
1 bunch of fresh oregano, leaves picked
1 garlic clove, minced
juice of 1 lemon
120ml (4fl oz/½ cup) extra virgin olive oil
sea salt, to taste

Wash the fennel and remove the top
green stalks; I like to keep a few of the
fronds to garnish. Thinly slice the fennel
into crescents and place in a mixing bowl
with the pomegranate seeds and oregano
and set aside. Crush the garlic with salt
and combine with the lemon juice and
extra virgin olive oil. Add the dressing to
the salad bowl and toss gently with your
hands. To serve, pile on a flat plate with
raised sides. Serve immediately.

Up to two days before

* Prepare the filling for the vegetarian vine leaves as well as the leaves
* Roll and stuff the vine leaves, assemble in the pot and keep in the fridge overnight, covered, to cook the next day
* Soak the chickpeas for the *moghrabieh*
* Boil the *moghrabieh* pearls, drain, leave to cool and store in an airtight container in the fridge
* Roast the peppers, cool, peel and drain, then store in an airtight container in the fridge
* Roast the walnuts, leave to cool, then and store in an airtight container

The day before

* Place the vine leaves on the stove, add the cooking juices and cook, then leave to cool and place in the fridge overnight
* Boil the chickpeas, leave to cool, then cover and place in the fridge
* Make the *muhammara*, then store in an airtight container in the fridge
* Wash and boil the *hindbeh*, strain well and place in an airtight container in the fridge
* Blitz the tomatoes, soak the bulgur wheat and make the *kammouneh* mixture, then place in separate airtight containers in the fridge
* Wash all the ingredients for the *ejjeh*, leave to dry completely, then place in an airtight container in the fridge
* Boil the *moghrabieh* pearls and leave to cool before placing in an airtight container in the fridge

On the day

* Prepare the mixture for the *ejjeh* and set aside
* Make the *tarator* and set aside
* Take out the vine leaves from the fridge and bring to room temperature
* Finely chop the onions for the *hindbeh*, salt and set aside
* Chop the salad ingredients for the *kammounet banadoura*, add to the bulgur wheat and tomato mixture and finish the dish, then plate and serve
* Finely chop the fennel and prepare all the ingredients for the salad, keep the dressing in a small bowl and set aside
* Make the *moghrabieh* and plate ready to serve
* Fry the onions, add the *hindbeh*, cook, then plate and serve
* Plate the *muhammara*, garnish and serve
* Flip the pot of vine leaves, garnish and serve
* Fry the *ejjeh*, one by one, plate and serve alongside the *tarator*
* Dress the fennel salad and serve

Lammet Al' Jiran

The Neighbourhood

There was always a sense of theatre and drama when it came to Mum's weekend spreads; food was a multi-sensory experience, which added so much life, excitement and joy to eating as a family. At almost any Lebanese family gathering, proudly and unassumingly in the middle of any weekend spread, you will see a platter of *Riz a Djej* (rice with chicken). Whether made by the host or brought by a guest, its presence evokes feelings of nostalgia and celebration.

My grandparents had no intention of leaving Lebanon in 1976, despite the unimaginable chaos of the civil war. Their home and their thriving sweet shop were in Tripoli, built up from selling trays of toffee in the poorer suburbs to employing close to 50 men; retirement was only one more Eid away. Their eldest daughters were amongst the first females to graduate from university, and the younger enrolled in private French schools. Finally, *tayta* packed a few bags, gathered her six youngest children and journeyed to Sydney, heartbroken.

As the adrenaline of fleeing war evaporated, the family had to cope with settling into what seemed like a lifetime of crippling chaos, and my *tayta* found herself sick with nausea at the prospect of never returning to Lebanon and slowly slipped into a deep depression. She had spent her early life escaping poverty and built a life rich in community and connection, and more than anything she longed for the women she turned to when she was in need. Her family had grown up in apartment buildings so close that you could hand the neighbour in the adjacent building a cup of sugar through the window. Food was exchanged and shared, delivered by the children from one neighbour to another. It was impossible to ignore the aromas that intertwined down the staircase.

And so it was food that was central to surviving and recreating a sense of home in my *tayta's* new reality in Australia, where the kitchen seemed to be the only place she could restore any peace, and where she retreated in a bid to recreate at least the smell and taste of home. It was then that food became a love language when no other language seemed to make sense.

Fundamental to those aromas was one of the key ingredients of Lebanese cooking, Sabaa Bharat (page 20) – cinnamon, clove, coriander and cumin, allspice, nutmeg and black pepper. While dishes like *Riz a Djej* carried the nostalgia and made use of ingredients *tayta* was easily able to acquire; the tender chicken atop flavoursome rice.

Mum prefers to cook this classic recipe with poussins – plump and proud, the skins a rich golden, caramel colour. Opening the small chickens was like opening a present to reveal a stuffing of bay leaves, cinnamon, carrots and celery hearts, their aromas sending us into a kind of delicious hypnosis. It was here I understood how Mum honoured the old traditional recipes while adding her own twists.

Left and below
ardishowkeh bil feren

Ardishowkeh bil Feren
Oven-roasted Artichokes

Eat these by pulling away the leaves, dipping them in the dressing and biting the bottom part of the leaf that was connected to the heart, collecting the flesh with your teeth. Work your way into the centre, remove the choke and finally eat the flesh. It's both an activity and an art and the perfect way to set the mood for lunch.

6 artichoke hearts

For the dressing/marinade
4 garlic cloves, crushed
250ml (8½fl oz/1 cup) mild olive oil
juice of 2 lemons
3 tbsp pomegranate molasses
sea salt, to taste
260ml (8½fl oz/1 cup) water

Wash the artichokes and remove the stems as well as any discoloured lower leaves. Using scissors, trim the tips of the thick petals from around the artichoke as well as about 2cm (¾in) from the tips, then place the artichokes in a container with ice and cold water. Place in the fridge for at least 2 hours or ideally overnight.

Preheat your oven to 200°C/400°F (gas 7).

Place all the dressing ingredients in a bowl and combine. Once the artichokes have finished soaking, remove from the water, place them in a baking dish and pour over the dressing, starting in each of the hearts and then pouring the remainder in the baking dish. Cover with baking parchment and foil and place in the oven, reduce the temperature to 180°C/350°F (gas 6), and bake for 60–80 minutes, checking after an hour. They are ready when the outer leaves come off easily.

Remove the artichokes and plate them, reserving the dressing in a small bowl.

Farouj Mahshi
Stuffed Poussins

Mum's ode to *Riz a Djej* using poussins as the star of the spread made her quite famous amongst our family and friends. The flesh is tender and juicy from the vegetable stuffing, and the Vegemite gives it a wonderful golden coat and an irresistible saltiness to the skin. It really doesn't matter if you haven't cooked with poussins before, treat them like small whole chickens, and trust the process.

6 quality poussins
1 lemon
125g (4oz/1 cup) plain (all-purpose) flour
1 tbsp Sabaa Bharat (page 20)
1 tbsp paprika, plus a pinch
2 tbsp ghee
1 tbsp Vegemite
12 Dutch carrots (not too large and thick)
a few celery stalks
2 tbsp olive oil
a handful of bay leaves (fresh or dried)
1 bulb of garlic, separated into cloves
3 cinnamon sticks, halved lengthways
sea salt, to taste
Rez w' Lahme (page 161), to serve

Begin by thoroughly washing the poussins and placing them in a large mixing bowl. Cut the lemon into wedges and squeeze the juice into the bowl, add a spoonful of the flour and begin to massage the poussins well for a minute. Rinse under cold running water, removing any excess fat from the cavity. They should feel clean and not have a slimy texture.

Place the poussins in a large mixing bowl and sprinkle with a little more of the flour along with the *bharat*, paprika, some salt and the ghee. Massage them well and, using your finger, evenly distribute the Vegemite over the skin and gently rub along the surface.

Place the carrots and celery in a mixing
bowl with some salt, the pinch of paprika
and the olive oil and massage well. Insert
2 carrots into each poussin cavity, along
with 1–2 pieces of celery, 1–2 bay leaves,
1 garlic clove and a halved cinnamon
stick. The vegetables and aromatics will
be sticking out of the poussins; this is fine.
Using cooking string, cross the legs and
tie them together to hold in all the flavour
and moisture. Place them in a baking dish
large enough to fit them comfortably and
place in the fridge for at least 2 hours
to marinate.

Preheat the oven to 190°C/375°F (gas 6).
Add 250ml (8½fl oz/1 cup) of water to the
base of the baking dish and place the tray
on the middle rack. Bake for about 1 hour,
or until the chicken is cooked and the
liquid has reduced and thickened slightly.

To serve, place the chicken on, or
alongside, a bed of *rez w' lahme*.

Rez w' Lahme
Spiced Rice with Mince and Nuts

**This spiced rice is a heavenly base for
the poussins and the juicy lamb mince
speckled throughout keeps it incredibly
moist and flavoursome. Weekend spreads
call for abundance and I love adorning the
rice with different types of nuts.**

720g (1lb 9½oz/4 cups) long-grain
  Sella rice
1 tbsp Sabaa Bharat (page 20)
1 tbsp ground cinnamon
½ tsp ground cloves
½ tsp ground black pepper
500g (1lb 2oz) coarse minced (ground)
  lamb or beef, or a mixture
4 tbsp ghee
50g (2oz/⅓ cup) pine nuts
50g (2oz/⅓ cup) halved almonds
40g (1½oz/⅓ cup) cashews
sea salt, to taste

Begin by washing the rice well, as
described on page 23, then place in
a mixing bowl along with all the spices
and some salt, combine well and set
aside. Place a heavy-based saucepan on
a high heat and add the mince, breaking
it up with a wooden spoon, and cook
until the meat has turned a light brown
and the juices are still in the pan. Add
1 tablespoon of ghee and the rice along
with 1.4 litres (50fl oz/6 cups) of water,
cover the pan and bring to the boil, then
turn it to low heat and simmer for about
35 minutes or until the rice is cooked.

As the rice is cooking, add the remaining
ghee to a small frying pan (skillet) along
with the pine nuts and fry until golden.
Remove with a slotted spoon and add to
a bowl. Repeat with the other nuts. Once
you have finished frying the nuts, tip any
ghee from the pan on top of the rice.

Place the rice on a large serving dish and
garnish with the fried nuts.

When I close my eyes, I can see myself at my *tayta*'s crowded house, bowl clutched in hand, waiting in line for a large scoop of rice, the warm aroma of cinnamon making me hop on the spot in anticipation. I see this same giddiness in my daughters, Layla and Eden.

Below *farouj mahshi*

Salata Arabiyeh
Arabic Chopped Salad

This salad generally includes whatever is in season or is growing in the garden at the time. We are very lucky as my father-in-law has one of those lemon trees that fruits throughout the year, so every few weeks he drops off a box of freshly picked lemons, leaves still intact – so good, we peel the outer skin and eat them as you would an orange, dipped in some salt. The finely diced lemon gives this salad plenty of acidity, truly complementing the *rez w' lahme*. I usually scoop up the two together for the perfect mouthful.

1 bunch of mint
2 bunches of flat-leaf parsley
500g (1lb 2oz) cherry tomatoes
4 Lebanese cucumbers
1 large Spanish onion
1 lemon, very finely diced, skin and all
120ml (4fl oz/½ cup) lemon juice
120ml (4fl oz/½ cup) extra virgin olive oil
sea salt, to taste

Wash the fresh herbs and leave them to dry before finely chopping them. Cut the tomatoes and cucumbers into small dice, the Spanish onion (and lemon) slightly finer. Season the salad with salt, lemon juice and extra virgin olive oil and combine all the ingredients with your hands. Serve immediately.

Batata Harra
Chilli Coriander Potatoes

The roasted potatoes we grew up on varied slightly to the traditional fried version. Mum always found ways to make dishes easier when preparing a whole spread, while still nodding to the origins of the dish. My advice is to make more than you need, as there never seems to be enough for everyone.

1kg (2lb 4oz) baby new potatoes
60ml (2fl oz/¼ cup) olive oil

For the dressing
3 garlic cloves
½ bunch of coriander (cilantro), roughly
  chopped including stalks
½ tsp paprika
1 tsp Aleppo chilli
2 tbsp olive oil
zest and juice of ½ lemon
sea salt, to taste

Wash the potatoes well and boil until they have slightly softened; you should be able to pierce them with a knife but they should not be totally cooked through.

Preheat your oven to 180°C/350°F (gas 5).

Remove the potatoes from the heat and cut them in halves or quarters depending on the size, then place in a mixing bowl. Pour over the oil, sprinkle with salt and toss well to combine. Transfer to a baking dish and bake for about 30 minutes until they begin to crisp. Turn the heat up to 200°C/400°F (gas 7) and bake for a further 15 minutes.

Crush the garlic with some salt in a pestle and mortar, then add the coriander and all the remaining dressing ingredients except the lemon zest, mixing to combine well. Once the potatoes have finished roasting, add the dressing to the baking dish and shake the dish to marry the juices. Garnish with the lemon zest and serve.

Loubiyeh Arida bil Zayt

Continental Beans Braised in
Tomato and Oil

You can prepare this a few hours ahead of
time and eat it at room temperature. I love
it the next day straight from the fridge
in a *laffeh* (wrap) with fresh herbs and
spring onion.

1.5kg (3lb 5oz) continental (helda)
  flat beans
250ml (8½fl oz/1 cup) olive oil
2 onions, cut into wedges
4 garlic cloves, sliced
4 tomatoes, diced
1 heaped tbsp tomato purée (paste)
1 tbsp pomegranate molasses
1 tsp Sabaa Bharat (page 20)
½ tsp chilli powder (optional)
sea salt, to taste

Begin by removing the tops and tails of
the beans and breaking them into 4cm
(1¼in) lengths. Wash them well and
set aside. In a heavy-based saucepan,
heat the oil, add the onions and fry until
they begin to colour. Add the garlic and
tomatoes and cook until fragrant and the
onions and garlic are slightly translucent,
then add the tomato purée, pomegranate
molasses, spices and salt. Continue to
cook for about 30 minutes.

Add the beans and toss the pan until they
are covered in the sauce.

Add 250ml (8½fl oz/1 cup) of water,
cover and cook for 20 minutes on a
medium–high heat. Uncover and
continue to cook for about 15 minutes,
tossing every 5 minutes. Serve warm
or at room temperature.

Mutabbal Hamwi
Syrian Layered Aubergine Dip

This recipe came from our neighbour Mona, who grew up in Hama in Syria, her childhood home built along the river. A wonderful cook, she would make this layered dish whenever she came to one of our gatherings. It has lived on in our spreads ever since.

For the *mutabbal*
4 medium-sized aubergines (eggplants)
3 garlic cloves
120ml (4fl oz/½ cup) tahini
juice of 1 lemon
1 heaped tbsp Greek yogurt

For the topping
2 heaped tbsp ghee
50g (2½oz/⅓ cup) pine nuts
250g (9oz) lamb backstrap or lamb
   shoulder or tenderloin, finely diced
1 tbsp tomato purée (paste)
½ tsp Sabaa Bharat (page 20)
a pinch of ground black pepper
2 tomatoes, finely chopped
1 tsp Aleppo chilli
½ pomegranate, deseeded

You will need an exposed flame for this recipe to char the skin and build the smoky flavour; this can be done over a barbecue or on a gas stove. Alternatively, you can use an oven on a high heat, 220°C/425°F (gas 9), for about 45 minutes. You will achieve the texture but not the smoky flavour.

Wash the aubergines and, using a sharp knife, poke all over. Place over a flame until the skin is charred and flaking off, turning them regularly. Repeat with all the aubergines, then place in a colander over a bowl to cool slightly before peeling.

Place the aubergines under cold running water, hold the stalk and peel off the skin. Take care not to remove too much flesh with the skin. Remove the tops with a knife and leave the peeled aubergines to strain further in the colander while you prepare the rest of the dish.

To make the *mutabbal* (smoky aubergine dip) crush the garlic with some salt in a mixing bowl and add the tahini and lemon juice, then begin to incorporate with a spoon. Add the yogurt and combine until you have reached a smooth, creamy paste. Taste for salt and lemon. Add the aubergine flesh and, using a pestle, beat into the tahini mixture until you have a smooth but textured dip. Set aside.

To make the topping, in a frying pan (skillet), melt half of the ghee, add the pine nuts and fry until golden brown, remove from the heat and set aside in a separate bowl.

Add the diced lamb to the same frying pan (skillet) and cook until caramelized and any moisture has evaporated. Add the remaining tablespoon of ghee, and allow it to sizzle before adding the tomato purée, *bharat*, black pepper, Aleppo chilli and finally the tomatoes. Let them cook and combine together for a few minutes. Toss in three-quarters of the pine nuts and set aside.

To serve, place the aubergine dip on a serving dish and spread with the back of a spoon. Flatten the middle, put the meat and sauce on top and spread evenly. Garnish with the remaining pine nuts and pomegranate seeds.

A day ahead

* Wash, marinate and stuff the poussins, then set aside in the fridge, covered with foil
* Fry the nuts for the rice, leave to cool, then set aside in the fridge in an airtight container
* Fry the mince for the rice, leave to cool and set aside in the fridge in an airtight container
* Chargrill the aubergines, drain and cool, then set aside in the fridge in an airtight container
* Prepare the beans, ready to be cooked the next day, then set aside in the fridge
* Wash all the *salata arabiyeh* ingredients, leave to dry and return to the fridge
* Finely dice the lamb and set aside in the fridge
* Prepare the artichokes, submerge in ice-cold water and place in the fridge overnight
* Make the dressing for the artichokes and place in an airtight container in the fridge

On the day

* Remove the aubergines from the fridge, place in a strainer and leave them to come back to room temperature
* Roast the artichokes
* Boil the potatoes, then set aside
* Prepare the *salata arabiyeh* ingredients, place the dressing in a small bowl and set aside in the fridge
* Make the dressing for the potatoes and set aside
* Remove the artichokes, plate and serve
* Place the poussins in the oven
* Bake the potatoes
* Add the meat to a pot and prepare the rice – once it is ready keep in the pot, covered, to stay warm
* Prepare the beans and place in a serving dish
* Prepare the sauce for the *mutabbal hamwi* and set aside to cool slightly
* Finish preparing the *mutabbal*, top with the sauce and serve
* Dress the salad and place in a serving dish
* Place the rice on a serving dish and either pull apart some of the poussins to decorate or serve alongside
* Toss the potatoes in the dressing, plate and serve immediately

Mashawi

The Barbecue

The scent of traditional Lebanese barbecues is
known to travel a fair distance, and in every Lebanese
family home there is a designated barbecue area
to accommodate everyone sitting around to cook
and eat.

For my husband's parents, Houda and Naji, who arrived in Australia in the late 1960s, barbecues would become a weekend ritual. Houda and Naji's weekdays were spent working tirelessly in factories and, armed with a small Arabic-to-English translation book, Houda was able to converse with the local Australians and began to navigate her way around. Meticulous about where to source her meat, Houda was grateful when she heard of a local Lebanese butcher. Lamb was one of the cheapest things to eat in Australia, unlike Lebanon where it was an occasional delicacy. Most importantly, there was refrigeration and constant electricity in Australia, so you could freeze meat for storage.

After overhearing a colleague at the factory talking about her weekend spent fishing in Narrabeen, and barbecuing by the sea, Houda couldn't wait for the end of the working week. The preparation for the barbecue began several days in advance.

When they arrived at Lake Narrabeen there were small fire places, or *mawehdeh* in Arabic, set up all over the park by previous visitors. The national parks were filled with migrant families basking in the sunshine and beauty, treasuring all that the new country had to offer. So much was missing yet, somehow, the days spent barbecuing and fishing after a long week of work would make up their fondest memories. At the farmers' markets, they bought a plethora of ingredients they missed – such as aubergines, parsley, beans and Lebanese cucumbers – and so the barbecue spread began to expand, from meat skewers to dips, salads and, most importantly, Lebanese bread.

Our family only needs the slightest excuse to barbecue – it is one of our favourite ways to gather and eat at the weekend, as is the case for most Lebanese families all over the world. Although often there is no particular occasion, the sense of celebration is in the air and as the guests begin to arrive, so does the excitement. My dad would leave the house early to be the first person at the butcher to get the pick of the meat. He would bring home boneless lamb shoulder that Mum would trim and cut up for the meat skewers, weaving thin pieces of fat between the flesh of the meat. Coarsely ground mince was made into *kafta*. Finally, a piece of liver that would also be skewered and, once cooked, wrapped tightly in a wrap with freshly squeezed lemon juice and chilli. Side dishes would change with the season but always included zesty salads – never only one – using the best of what was in season, plus freshly made dips, the *baba ghanouj* still warm from the hot charcoals. Mum's signature fresh garlic and chilli oil made the best dipping sauce for the charcoal wings and thick-cut potato slices which, slathered between pieces of Lebanese bread, were cooked on the fire.

Preparing the Barbecue

In Arabic, a charcoal barbecue is called a *man'al* or *kanoun*, depending on what region you are from. A rack sits above to rest the meat and skewers. The char of the meat and the smoky charcoal flavour is what Lebanese barbecues are famous for.

According to my friend Bader, who is one of the best barbecuers I know, preparing a charcoal barbecue is not as simple as just getting a barbecue nice and hot and throwing your meat on to cook. He was kind enough to share with me what is otherwise considered top-secret information.

Things you Need

A classic steel Lebanese barbecue grill (you can also use a Webber-style)
Lebanese charcoal mangrove-style coals (barbecue briquettes are a good alternative, but any barbecue charcoal should also work, though will result in less authentic flavours)
Firelighter cubes to ignite the charcoals
A flat-surfaced, solid hand paddle

First and foremost, set up your barbecue in an open outdoor area away from any flammable nearby objects.

Set Up the Charcoals

To light the charcoals evenly, you want to first start by placing the individual pieces in a triangle stack. You want to have each of the small charcoal logs stacked to form a pyramid shape. This will allow the air to flow in and below the charcoals and direct the heat up towards the highest point. As the charcoals catch alight you will see the heat naturally force the flame up, distributing the fire evenly.

Light the Charcoals

There are various ways you can spark a flame on charcoals and the best method is always using a slow-burning fire starter, such as fire lighter cubes. These cubes will light with a traditional lighter and continue to provide a flame to ignite the charcoals. Place a few cubes at the bottom of the pyramid stack and ignite them.

Help the Flame

You often find Lebanese men standing around a barbecue taking turns in helping the flame catch fire by waving a paddle. Continue to wave the paddle until you see a decent-sized flame wrapping the charcoal pyramid shape. Repeat the wave when you see the flame die down and stop when you have sufficient flame. At some point, depending on the amount of charcoals you have used, this should typically take 15–20 minutes.

Know When the Charcoals Are Ready

The simplest way to know when charcoals are ready is to look for when the centre of the charcoal pyramid has turned to grey surface ash. The outside of the pyramid should remain black – you don't need to wait for the entire pyramid to fully light and turn grey, as the fire will then be too hot for the meat. If the logs are already fully lit, then it is likely the charcoals will not last the full distance to complete the cooking cycle.

Cook the Meat

When you're ready to start cooking, spread the charcoals to cover the cooking area but ensure the charcoal logs are still touching each other, leaving no gaps. Ideally you want to have enough to cover most of the barbecue floor area with at least one layer and a few coals spread around on top of the layer so there aren't any cold spots. Once you have spread them, leave them for 5 minutes to burn further and form an almost white layer of ash on top.

If you are using a traditional steel Lebanese barbecue, your skewers should sit vertically on each side of the tray. This will balance the skewers well and give you a rotational point to flip the meat to each side once cooked. If you are using a Webber-style barbecue, you will need the grill inserted to hold the meat away from the charcoals. The best method to follow when rotating the skewers is 7–4–3. The first side should take about 7 minutes to cook and turn golden brown. You should then rotate the skewer a third of the way to one side and let it cook for 4 minutes, and the final rotation should be 3 minutes. This is an approximate time and is best judged by the colour of the meat. Not all skewers will cook at the same pace, particularly those on the outer edges. You should leave the slightly undercooked side for a little longer.

For chicken pieces and other meats placed directly on the barbecue, follow a simple 10–7 rule, whereby one side is left to cook for 10 minutes or so until golden brown, then flipped to the other side for a slightly shorter cooking time. Chicken is traditionally put on first as it takes the longest to cook, followed by other meats and *kafta*, which is the quickest.

Left cooking the *kafta* and
lahme mishwiyeh
Below preparing the *kafta*

At our barbecues we rarely sit around the table.
Instead, there is an organic movement of people
from the food table back to the barbecue, a
sequence of filling your plate with salads and dips
and making your way back to the barbecue to eat
the meat as soon as it comes off the fire.

Lahme Mishwiyeh
Lamb Skewers

Boneless lamb shoulder makes for the best cut of lamb to barbecue; the meat is incredibly tender and the fat caramelizes into salty, juicy deliciousness. If you can't find pickling onions, just use small brown onions cut into quarters. You will need wooden or metal skewers for these.

1.5kg (3lb 5oz) boneless lamb shoulder
sea salt, to taste
8–10 small pickling onions, skinned
    and halved

Often Lebanese butchers will have ready-diced lamb shoulder or will dice the meat for you. If not, cut the meat into 2cm (½in) cubes and sprinkle generously with salt – this is the only seasoning. If you are using wooden skewers, soak them in water for at least an hour to prevent charring. Thread about 6 meat cubes onto each skewer, placing a halved onion in the middle, or more depending on your preference. Place on a hot barbecue for about 5 minutes or as desired, turning over when one side is cooked. Serve immediately.

Kafta Mishwiyeh
Homemade Kafta Skewers

Making your own *kafta* meat is incredibly satisfying, as it is so versatile. You can put it on skewers, which is how we prepare it for barbecues, or flatten it into hamburger patties and cook in a frying pan (skillet); it also freezes very well. You will need wooden or metal skewers for these.

1kg (2lb 4oz) fine minced (ground) lamb
1 large onion, very finely chopped
1 bunch of parsley, finely chopped
1 heaped tsp Sabaa Bharat (page 20)
sea salt, to taste
1 tsp paprika

Add all the ingredients to a mixing bowl and combine well with your hands. Have a small bowl of water beside you to wet your hands and, using a small ball of *kafta* meat, press the skewer into the ball and mould and stretch the *kafta* along the skewer until about 2cm (½in) thick and about 12cm (4½in) long.

Place on a hot barbecue for about 5 minutes or as desired, turning over when one side is cooked. Serve immediately.

Kibbeh Mekliyeh
Fried Kibbeh

Mum's barbecues always began with a platter of *kibbeh* and *sambousek* – another excuse to gather people in the kitchen.

Makes 55 pieces

For the filling
800g (1lb 12oz) coarse minced (ground) lamb or beef
500g (1lb 2oz) brown onions, finely chopped
1 heaped tsp Sabaa Bharat (page 20)
1 heaped tbsp ghee
75g (2½oz/½ cup) pine nuts
1 bunch of parsley, finely chopped
2 tbsp pomegranate molasses
sea salt, to taste

For the *kibbeh* dough (outer casing)
580g (1lb 4½oz/3½ cups) fine brown bulgur wheat
1 tsp Sabaa Bharat (page 20)
2 tbsp plain (all-purpose) flour
1 large brown onion, quartered
¼ wedge of red (bell) pepper
1 sprig of basil
1 sprig of marjoram
2 sprigs of mint
1 heaped tbsp Kammouneh (page 20)
500g (1lb 12oz) minced (ground) *kibbeh* meat (a combination of beef and lamb, see recipe introduction on page 116)
sea salt, to taste
vegetable oil, for frying

Wash the bulgur in a mixing bowl until the water runs clear. Soak for 30 minutes and then strain as much water as possible with your hands. (This step is crucial.)

For the filling, place the meat in a large frying pan (skillet) on a medium heat and break it up with a wooden spoon, cooking until all the moisture has evaporated. Add the onions, season with salt and add the *bharat*. Leave to cook until translucent and the moisture has evaporated.

In a small separate frying pan, add the ghee and pine nuts and toast until just golden, then remove from the heat. Add the parsley, pine nuts and ghee and pomegranate molasses to the meat and mix well. Set aside to cool.

Once the bulgur has expanded, season with salt and *bharat*, add the flour and mix.

Add the onion, red pepper, herbs and spices to a food processor and season with salt. Add a cup of the fluffy bulgur and pulse until well combined. Add to the bulgur mixture and mix well.

Add the *kibbeh* meat to the bulgur and begin to massage in the meat. I scoop a handful and slide it between my palms to really incorporate the two elements well, and then knead until you have a *kibbeh* dough. Have a bowl of water handy to help massage all the ingredients together to form a soft and pliable dough.

To assemble each *kibbeh* ball, moisten your palm with water, break off 40g (1½oz) of dough and roll it into a ball. The aim is to produce a thin, even, 4mm thick meat shell for your filling. Place the ball in one hand and insert your index finger into the ball, being careful not to pierce through. If you do, start again or mend with some water and the tips of your fingers. Begin to rotate the ball, pressing on the internal wall until you have a hollow egg shape. Place 1 tablespoon of filling into the opening, pushing the filling in slightly with your finger to enable you to close it. Cup your hands to close the ball into an egg shape with a slightly pointy tip.

To cook, heat enough oil in a frying pan (skillet) so that the *kibbeh* are three-quarters submerged. Fry in small batches. Check the oil temperature by inserting the tip of the *kibbeh*, it should fizzle around it. Once they have cooked, about 3–4 minutes, remove with a slotted spoon and leave to drain on a plate lined with paper towels to absorb any residual oil.

Sambousek
Fried Hand Pies

Sambousek are always made in advance. They are then frozen and taken out to fry on the day. Freeze uncooked pies by laying them on a flat surface in the freezer for an hour. Once hardened, you can place them in a freezer bag on top of one another.

Makes about 50

For the dough
500g (1lb 2oz) plain (all-purpose) flour
2 tbsp cornflour (cornstarch)
1 tsp salt
1 tsp caster (superfine) sugar
2 heaped tbsp ghee, slightly melted
2 tbsp milk
250–300ml (8½–10fl oz/1–1½ cups) water
neutral oil, for frying

For the meat filling
350g (12oz) lamb mince (or beef)
2 medium-sized brown onions, finely diced
1 tsp Sabaa Bharat (page 20)
1 heaped tbsp ghee
3 tbsp pine nuts
1 tbsp pomegranate molasses
sea salt, to taste

For the cheese filling
240g (8oz/2 cups) grated mozzarella
120g (4oz/1 cup) grated halloumi
60g (3oz/½ cup) cubed feta
1 heaped tsp nigella seeds

To make the dough, sift the flour into a large mixing bowl along with the cornflour, salt, sugar and ghee. Rub the mixture with your fingers until you have a loose crumb. Add the milk and 250ml (8½fl oz/1 cup) of water and begin to incorporate with your hands to bring it together, adding small extra amounts of water, if necessary. Knead for a few minutes until soft, then cover and leave to rest for 1 hour.

Begin working on the meat filling. Place the meat in a medium-sized frying pan

(skillet) and break up with a wooden spoon, cooking on a medium heat until all the moisture has evaporated. Add the onions and *bharat*, season with salt and leave the onions to cook with the meat until translucent and the moisture has evaporated. In a separate small frying pan (skillet), add the ghee and pine nuts and toast until golden, being mindful not to burn them – they will continue cooking in the residual heat of the ghee. Add the pomegranate molasses and the pine nuts to the meat and leave the mixture to cool.

For the cheese filling, mix the cheeses with the nigella seeds.

Once the dough has rested, cut it into quarters and cover with a cloth, while you work on the first quarter. Roll it out into a 3mm thick sheet and cut out about 12 circles using a 9cm (3½in) round cookie cutter. Roll the excess into a ball and place under the cloth while you fill the first batch.

I find the dough shrinks slightly when cut, so I gently roll it out to maintain a 3mm thickness. Avoid holes or the filling will burst out when frying. Place a heaped teaspoon of your chosen filling in the centre and close it up by folding the half circle over, encasing the filling and creating a crescent shape. To differentiate between the two fillings, use a fork to press the edges shut for one and use your fingers to fold over the hem in small diagonal pleats around the curve for the other; this will also help to secure the filling when cooking.

To cook, heat enough oil in a frying pan so that the *sambousek* are submerged and fry in small batches. Check the oil temperature by inserting the tip of the *sambousek* – it should fizzle around it. Once they are golden, after 3–4 minutes, remove with a slotted spoon and leave to drain on a plate with some paper towels to absorb any residual oil. Serve hot or at room temperature.

You could also marinate chicken breast or chicken thighs following the same method as for *jawaneh w' toum*, just thread the meat onto skewers – we call this *shish tawouk*.

Jawaneh w' Toum
Mum's Chicken Wings and Chilli Garlic
Dipping Sauce

I could well and truly eat a bucket of
these, especially with mum's chilli garlic
dipping sauce, which we call *toum*.

3kg (6lb 10oz) chicken wings
1 lemon
1 tbsp plain (all-purpose) flour

For the marinade
juice of 2 lemons
zest of 1 lemon
olive oil
4 garlic cloves, minced
1 heaped tbsp Greek yogurt
1 tbsp paprika
sea salt, to taste

For the *toum*
6 garlic cloves
1 long red chilli
1 long green chilli
120ml (4fl oz/½ cup) lemon juice
180ml (6fl oz/¾ cup) extra virgin olive oil
sea salt, to taste

Begin by thoroughly washing the wings
and placing them in a mixing bowl. Cut
the lemon into wedges and squeeze the
juice onto the wings, adding the flour and
massaging well. Rinse the wings under
cold running water until they feel clean
and don't have a slimy texture.

Place the wings in a bowl along with all
the marinade ingredients. Massage and
set aside to marinate for at least 4 hours.

To make the *toum*, place the garlic with
some salt in a mortar and crush well.
Roughly chop the chillies, add to the
mortar and crush. Transfer to a small
bowl, add the lemon juice and olive oil and
mix well.

Place the wings on a hot barbecue for
about 5–7 minutes, turning to ensure all
sides are brown and the chicken is cooked
through. Serve immediately with the *toum*.

Baba Ghanouj
Charred Aubergine and Tahini Dip

Everyone's favourite, charred, smoky and
moreish dip.

3 medium-sized seedless aubergines
  (eggplants)
2 garlic cloves
120ml (4fl oz/½ cup) tahini
juice of 1 lemon
1 heaped tbsp Greek yogurt
sea salt, to taste

To serve
a handful of pomegranate seeds
a handful of chopped oregano or parsley
a drizzle of extra virgin olive oil

You will need an exposed flame for this
recipe to char the skin and build the smoky
flavour – this can be done on a barbecue
or over a gas stove. Alternatively, you can
use an oven on maximum heat for about
45 minutes. You will achieve the texture
but not the smoky flavour.

Wash the aubergines and, using a sharp
knife, poke all over, then place over a
flame until the skin is charred and flaking
off. Turn regularly to cook all over, then
place in a colander to cool slightly. Place
each aubergine under cold running water,
holding onto the stalk and peeling off the
skin. Handle with care, holding it from the
plump end to avoid breakage. Remove
the tops with a knife and leave the peeled
aubergines to drain in the colander.

Crush the garlic with some salt in a mixing
bowl, add the tahini and lemon juice and
begin to incorporate with a spoon, then
add the yogurt and combine until you
have a smooth paste. Taste for salt and
lemon. Add the aubergine flesh and beat
with a pestle until you have a smoother,
textured, dip.

Garnish with the pomegranate seeds and
herbs and a drizzle of extra virgin olive oil.

Salatet Kabees Malfouf
Pickled Cabbage Salad

This quick pickled salad is what ties all the flavours and elements of the barbecue together.

1 tsp caraway seeds
¼ head of purple cabbage, finely shredded
60ml (4fl oz/¼ cup) apple cider vinegar
½ tsp caster (superfine) sugar
sea salt, to taste
60ml (4fl oz/¼ cup) extra virgin olive oil
juice of ½ lemon

Heat the caraway seeds in a frying pan (skillet) until fragrant, then remove from the heat. Add the remaining ingredients to a mixing bowl, along with the toasted caraway seeds. Toss the cabbage with the dressing, squeezing it gently to infuse. Serve immediately.

Batata Mishwiyeh
Barbecued Potato Chips

Once all the meat has been cooked, the last thing to go onto the barbecue is the sliced potatoes, perfect for dipping and how we always finish a barbecue.

700g (1lb 9oz) white potatoes
sea salt, to taste

Wash the potatoes well, keeping the skin on, slice them into 5mm (¼in) thick disks. Place in a bowl of salted water to soak, then place on a hot barbecue to char on each side. Serve immediately.

Salatet Za'atar w' Zaytoun
Wild Za'atar and Olive Salad

My friend Mona's family had a large patch of wild za'atar growing abundantly, very similar to how you would see it grow in Lebanon and when the season called for it, she would make this salad. If you have access to wild za'atar (or wild thyme as it's also called) use it here; alternatively, fresh oregano, as I often make do with, works just as well.

2 generous bunches of za'atar or oregano
100g (3½oz/1 cup) green olives, pitted and roughly chopped
1 Spanish onion, finely chopped
2 tbsp pomegranate molasses
60ml (2fl oz/¼ cup) lemon juice
60ml (2fl oz/¼ cup) extra virgin olive oil
sea salt, to taste

Wash and dry the herbs before picking off all the leaves and discarding the stems. Place in a mixing bowl along with the olives and onion. Make the dressing in a small bowl with the remaining ingredients and taste before adding to the salad and tossing well. Serve immediately.

Hummus bi Tahini
Chickpea and Tahini Dip

Balancing the flavours of hummus, with lemon, salt and tahini, far outweighs trying to achieve ultimate silkiness. It's just not what it's all about. If you want to use a can of chickpeas, simply tip the contents of the can into a saucepan and simmer for about 10 minutes.

350g (12oz/2 cups) dried chickpeas
  (garbanzos)
1 tsp bicarbonate of soda (baking soda)
250g (9oz/heaped 1 cup) tahini
100ml (3½fl oz/scant ½ cup) lemon juice
3 garlic cloves
50–100ml (2½fl oz/¼–½ cup) ice-cold
  water
sea salt, to taste

Prepare the chickpeas as described on page (22), extending the cooking time by 15 minutes, or until the chickpeas collapse easily but are not yet mushy.

Leave the chickpeas to cool slightly, then, while warm, drain them and transfer to a food processor and process them until a stiff paste forms. It is important they become a paste before you add any of the other ingredients. While the machine is still running, gradually add the tahini, lemon juice, garlic, and salt to taste. Once those ingredients have been processed and while the machine is still running, gradually drizzle in the ice-cold water slowly. Keep processing for another 3–5 minutes.

If you have made this in advance, place the hummus in the fridge once it has cooled and bring it back to room temperature when you wish to serve, otherwise set aside until required.

Salatet Emmi
Mum's Garden Salad

This chunky garden salad evolves with the seasons and relies on what is growing in the garden. Rocket (arugula) is a staple leafy green often found in Lebanese gardens and, when available, it is the hero of this salad, its peppery flavour elevated by the dill and sumac.

½ bunch of mint
½ bunch of parsley
a small handful of dill
2 bunches of rocket (arugula)
2 tomatoes
2 cucumbers
1 bunch of small radishes
1 small Spanish onion, finely sliced
1 tsp sumac
60ml (2fl oz/¼ cup) lemon juice
60ml (2fl oz/¼ cup) extra virgin olive oil
2 tbsp pomegranate molasses
sea salt, to taste

Wash and dry the herbs before picking off the leaves. Very roughly chop the mint, parsley and dill and add to a mixing bowl with the rocket. Chop the tomatoes, cucumber and radishes into large dice, then finely slice the onion and add to the bowl. In a small bowl, mix the sumac, lemon juice, olive oil and pomegranate molasses, mix well and add to the salad. Taste the salad for salt and serve immediately.

Salsa Mishwiyeh
Charred Vegetable Salsa

Although the elements of most Lebanese
barbecues are the same – meat, salads
and dips – there are some specialities you
adopt from people along the way, like this
salsa made of charred vegetables and
simply seasoned with sumac and salt
and a drizzle of olive oil. So simple and
yet so perfect.

2 medium-sized ripe tomatoes
2 small onions, peeled
2 green chillies
sea salt, to taste
¼ tsp sumac
a drizzle of extra virgin olive oil

Thread the tomatoes, onions and chillies
onto either metal or soaked wooden
skewers. Place on an exposed charcoal
barbecue until the vegetables have
charred and the skins are blistered
slightly. Remove from the skewers and
place onto a wooden board. Finely chop
the vegetables, combining them together
as you do so. Season with salt, sumac
and a drizzle of extra virgin olive oil.
Serve warm.

Right *batata mishwiyeh* and
salsa mishwiyeh

A few days before
* Soak the raw chickpeas overnight or defrost prepared chickpeas from the freezer
* Prepare the *sambousek* in advance and cook from frozen on the day)
* Prepare the *kibbeh* in advance and cook from frozen on the day)

The day before
* Boil the chickpeas, leave to cool, then make the hummus and store in an airtight container in the fridge
* Marinate the chicken, then store in an airtight container in the fridge
* Make the *toum*, then store in an airtight container in the fridge
* Wash all the fresh herbs and vegetables, dry and store in the fridge
* Prep the pickled cabbage salad and store in an airtight container in the fridge, with the dressing separate
* Deseed the pomegranate for the *baba ghanouj*, then store in an airtight container in the fridge
* Deseed and chop the olives for the salad, then store in an airtight container in the fridge
* Prepare the *kafta* mixture, put the mince on skewers and store in an airtight container in the fridge
* Prepare the lamb shoulder, place the meat on skewers and store in an airtight container in the fridge

On the day
* Prepare Mum's garden salad and the za'atar salad and store both in the fridge, with the dressing separate
* Prep the potatoes and place in a bowl of water until ready to cook
* Fry the *kibbeh* and *sambousek*, plate and serve
* Prepare the vegetables on skewers for the salsa; set aside
* Place the aubergines on a hot barbecue to char; once ready, prep the *baba ghanouj*, plate, garnish and serve
* Place the skewered vegetables on the barbecue to char; once ready, prep the salsa, plate and serve
* Plate the hummus, garnish and serve
* Dress cabbage salad plate and serve
* Cook the chicken first and place in a casserole dish until the remaining meat is cooked; plate and serve with *toum*
* Cook the meat and *kafta* (we usually line half of the barbecue with each so both can come off at the same time and then replenish)
* Dress the garden salad, plate and serve
* Dress the za'atar salad, plate and serve
* Finally, cook the potatoes on the barbecue and serve

Halawiyat

Bitter Sweet

As children, we often visited Lebanese sweet shops. My favourite one was renowned for making *bouza*, a slightly thicker, sticky Lebanese ice cream. We would stand in an endless queue to order the *mshakal* (mixed flavours), which included a thumb-sized scoop of every flavour in the counter, piled on top of a crispy cone. People travelled far and wide particularly for the famous *toot* (mulberry) and *laymoun* (lemon) flavours and eventually for the Lebanese sweets and pastries.

My grandfather, *jido* Ibrahim, was 73 years old when he finally surrendered to coming to Australia, accepting that, after five years of patiently waiting, the civil war that tore Lebanon apart had no end in sight. He arrived in the summer of 1981; the war would go on to last another thirteen years.

After years of selling sweets from a large steel tray around the poorer suburbs of Tripoli, my *jido* and *tayta* eventually opened their first sweet shop together in the souk. They set out to make the sweets they loved to eat, inexpensive desserts the townspeople could afford, a market that had not yet been catered for. They made *halawet al rez* (a sweet sticky rice) and *bouza* in the summer, and *sahlab w' haleeb* (sweet milk with cinnamon) and buckets of *haboub* (barley and aniseed porridge) in the winter.

After several years, their sweet offering ever-evolving, my grandparents began journeying to Syria, 45 minutes north of Tripoli, in search of nuts, spices and ingredients to use in their sweets. They were renowned for their *maamoul* (semolina biscuits) and, during the religious festivals – Eid Al Adha, Eid Al Fitr, Easter and Christmas – Mum and her siblings would sit around the table wrapping thousands of them.

Although my *jido* worked tirelessly, it was my *tayta* who was the mastermind behind the success of the business. As competition built around the souk, with sweet shops beginning to open all around the city, she knew one way to elevate their sweets and separate them from the rest. The waters orange blossom and rose are the dominant extracts used when flavouring Lebanese sweets, and the sweets would only ever be as good as the quality of the waters used.

As an experiment in the glass house on the flat roof of their apartment building, *tayta* built a distillery, and once a month the same strong, young man in gardening boots would march up the five flights of stairs with a twenty-kilo sack resting on his shoulder, stuffed to the seams with roses. He would put it down on a large cotton sheet laid out for him and catch his breath. The bags were so full that the roses would explode out when sliced open and Mum recalls the lingering scent of the roses on her tiny fingers.

My *tayta's* flower waters soon became the talk of the town and, with the community of women around her, she began supplying sweet shops, including my *jido's*, as people flocked to the souk to buy their artisinal sweets.

Lebanese sweet shops are renowned for their skill and expertise in making some of the finest desserts we Lebanese people are famous for, and it is custom to visit the sweet shop on the way to a gathering or celebration. There you will find *knafeh bi jibneh* (sweet cheese with a semolina crumb) kept warm in a large simmering pot, trays of freshly fried *znoud el sit* (crispy fried pastry filled with clotted cream), platters of *baklawa* and great mounds of *awamet* (syrup-soaked doughnuts).

The home cooks, however, had a few tricks up their sleeves too, with desserts made traditionally in the home for weekend gatherings, special occasions and religious festivities. After a long lunch, we would assemble a dessert table, with an assortment of sweets, those prepared at home and others brought from the sweet shop by our guests, along with platters of seasonal fruit to serve with tea and coffee – a sweet end to the day.

Maamoul
Semolina Biscuits Filled with Walnuts
and Pistachios

To this day, the tapping of the wooden
maamoul mould on the kitchen table is
one of my favourite sounds. My heart
knows exactly what is about to come.

Traditionally these are made in
generous quantities, as they are shared
amongst friends and family – this recipe
will make 3.5kg (7lb 10oz) of dough. This is
an ideal quantity to make both pistachio-
filled and walnut-filled *maamoul*, as the
dough is the same for both, although you
can halve the recipe if you wish. Keep for
up to 3 months in an airtight container in
a cool, dry place or in the fridge. You can
buy the oval wooden moulds in Middle
Eastern stores.

**Makes about 50 walnut and
50 pistachio *maamoul***

For the maamoul dough
1½ sachets of instant yeast
250ml (8½fl oz/1 cup) warm milk
1kg (2lb 4oz) fine semolina
1kg (2lb 4oz) coarse semolina
230g (8oz/1¼ cups) white caster
  (superfine) sugar
875g (1lb 14oz) good-quality unsalted
  butter, chopped or 600g (1lb 5oz) ghee
60ml (2fl oz/¼ cup) rosewater
180ml (6fl oz/¾ cup) orange
  blossom water
1 sachet *mahlab* (page 24, if you
  can source)
100g (3½oz/1 cup) ground almonds
icing (confectioners') sugar, for dusting

For the pistachio filling
500g (1lb 2oz/3⅓ cups) pistachios
185g (6½oz/1 cup) caster
  (superfine) sugar
80ml (3fl oz/⅓ cup) orange blossom
  water

For the walnut filling
500g (1lb 2oz/5 cups) walnuts
185g (6½oz/1 cup) caster
  (superfine) sugar
80ml (3fl oz/⅓ cup) orange blossom
  water

Add the yeast to the milk in a heatproof
bowl and place in the microwave for
1 minute, then leave to stand for a few
minutes, before adding this to a large
mixing bowl.

Add both of the semolinas and the sugar
to the bowl. Melt the butter or ghee very
lightly in the microwave so it is soft but
not fully melted, then add to the semolina.
Add the rosewater and orange blossom
water along with the *mahlab* (if using) to
the bowl, then the ground almonds before
finally adding the milk and yeast mixture.
Using your hands, begin to incorporate
all the ingredients together to form a
soft dough, rubbing the butter into the
semolina, kneading well and ensuring
all the ingredients have been combined
together. Leave to rest, covered with a
dish towel, in a cool, dry place for 4 hours.

Preheat the oven to 200°C/400°F (gas 7).

While your dough is resting, begin working
on your nut filling. Blitz the pistachios in a
food processor for a few seconds to break
them down slightly, then place in a mixting
bowl and repeat with the walnuts, placing
in a separate mixing bowl. It should be a
textured crumb, not very finely ground.
Add the sugar and orange blossom water
to each bowl of nuts and mix well. Set
aside with a teaspoon in each bowl.

Once your dough has rested for 4 hours,
knead it in the bowl with your hands to
loosen the mixture so that it will fit well
into your moulds.

Turn the oven down to 180°C/350°F (gas 6). Line a few baking trays with baking parchment. Take a small handful of dough (about 35g/1¼oz), roll it into a ball and place it in the palm of your hand. Put your finger in the ball and work the sides of the dough against the palm of your hand, rotating it as you go, to form a hollow pocket. Add a heaped teaspoon of your filling (about 15g/½oz) and then close the hole, making sure no filling is showing. The aim is to form a soft round ball to shape in your mould. Press the ball into the patterned side of the mould and gently tap the mould onto the clean surface to release your *maamoul*. Don't be discouraged if your first is not perfect. Repeat this until you have used all of your filling and dough. Sometimes there is a little bit of one or the other left over.

Place your *maamoul* on the baking trays and bake for 10–15 minutes until golden.

Do not handle the *maamoul* immediately as they will be very delicate while hot, but will firm up once they have cooled down. Once cool, use a flat spatula or scraper to remove from the tray.

If you are eating them straight away, dust generously with sifted icing sugar. If you are going to store them for later, put them in an airtight container somewhere cool and dark and dust before serving. They will keep for about 2 months.

Karbouj Halab
Syrian Meringue

This fabulous Syrian meringue is a simple way to transform a delicate biscuit into a show-stopper. My advice is to top your *maamoul* as you are serving.

550g (1lb 4oz/3 cups) white caster (superfine) sugar
1 tsp sea salt
1 tbsp lemon juice
2 egg whites
1 tsp vanilla bean paste
1 tbsp orange blossom water

To garnish
100g (3½oz/½ cup) crushed pistachios
rose petals

Begin by making the syrup. Put the sugar, 180ml (6fl oz/¾ cup) water and the salt into a small saucepan and bring to a light boil, stirring often. Add the lemon juice and let it boil for 5 minutes before reducing the heat for 10 minutes until the syrup thickens. Place the hot syrup in a heatproof jug with a spout or a teapot.

Place the egg whites and vanilla in a mixing bowl and beat with an electric mixer on high until stiff peaks form, about 6–7 minutes. While the mixer is running, add the orange blossom water followed by the hot syrup, drizzling it very slowly into the meringue. This should take about 10 minutes. By then, it should begin to thicken and be very glossy and not at all runny. Continue to mix until you are happy with the consistency. Set aside and leave to cool and set; it keeps well in the fridge once it is cooled.

To serve, use a spoon to ice the cooled *maamoul* with the meringue mixture. Garnish with ground pistachios and rose petals and serve immediately.

Nammoura
Semolina Slice Studded with Nuts

This version of *nammoura* is not as sweet as the store-bought kind. It is traditionally cut up into small diamond shapes with an almond in the centre of each, but somehow I didn't have enough almonds one day, so I used up all the nuts I did have and this was the result. Try it with ghee for a superb crumb.

120g (4oz/⅔ cup) caster (superfine) sugar
250g (9oz/2 cups) coarse semolina
250g (9oz/2 cups) fine semolina
275g (10oz) butter or ghee, melted
1 tbsp baking powder
300g (10½oz/1¼ cups) Greek yogurt
200g (7oz/1⅓ cups) mixed nuts, such as
   pistachios, almonds, cashews, walnuts

For the syrup
400g (14oz/2 cups) caster
   (superfine) sugar
1 tbsp lemon juice
1 tbsp orange blossom water

Preheat your oven to 180°C/350°F
(gas 6).

In a bowl, mix the sugar and semolinas. Reserve about 3 tablespoons of the butter or ghee and add the remainder to the bowl. Mix together, making sure the butter or ghee is well combined with the semolina. Add the baking powder to the yogurt before adding it to the semolina mixture. Mix thoroughly.

You can either use a rectangular baking dish or a round one. Line it with baking parchment and press the mixture in using the back of a wet spoon. Once the mixture is firmly pressed into the dish, press the nuts all around the top. If you would like to make the indentations and serve it traditionally, use a sharp wet knife to slice parallel lines about 2.5cm (1in) apart, then in the opposite direction until you have squares or diamonds. You can then place a blanched almond in the centre of each diamond. Once the nuts are slightly pressed into the *nammoura*, brush the remaining butter with a pastry brush all over the top.

Bake on the lowest rack in the oven for about 10–20 minutes and then move it up to the middle rack for another 15–20 minutes. How dark you like your *nammoura* is optional; some prefer it lightly coloured but I love it a dark, rich, golden colour, especially around the edges.

Meanwhile place the sugar and 240ml (8fl oz) water in a saucepan and simmer until the syrup thickens. Once it has slightly thickened, add the lemon juice and orange blossom water and leave to stand.

When the *nammoura* comes out of the oven, pour the hot syrup all over and watch it sizzle. Leave to cool completely before slicing into pieces.

Left and below preparing and
dusting *bascot bil tamer*

Bascot bil Tamer
Mum's Date Shortbread

This date shortbread is perfect with a strong Lebanese *ahweh* or *shai* (coffee or tea).

Makes about 50 biscuits

For the shortbread
900g (2lb/5 cups) self-raising (self-rising) flour
100g (3½oz/1 cup) ground almonds
½ tbsp *mahlab* (page 24, if you can source)
250ml (8½fl oz/1 cup) milk
250ml (8½fl oz/1 cup) vegetable oil or neutral oil
200g (7oz) butter softened

For the date filling
1kg (2lb 4oz) pitted dates in a bag (from a Lebanese grocer)
2 tbsp rosewater
2 tbsp orange blossom water
2 tbsp ghee or butter
icing (confectioners') sugar, for dusting

Start by preparing the dough, as it requires an hour to rest. You will need a large mixing bowl, as you will need to mix and knead the dough by hand in the bowl.

Sift the flour into the bowl, then add the ground almonds, *mahlab*, milk, oil and butter. Using clean hands, bring all the ingredients together to form a very soft dough. This shouldn't take too long and does not require rigorous kneading, just ensure all the butter has been worked into the flour and other wet ingredients.

Cover with a dish towel and leave to rest for 1 hour while you work on your filling. Preheat your oven to 180°C/350°F (gas 6).

For the filling, place the dates in a colander and wash with warm water. Place the washed dates in a deep tray along with the rosewater, orange blossom water and ghee. Bake until the dates are soft, about 5–10 minutes, but be careful not to burn or overcook them. Once they have softened well, mash them using a fork to combine them and form a thick, textured paste. Set aside to cool slightly.

Once the dates have cooled, have a small bowl of water handy, as your hands may get sticky from the mixture. Take a small handful of filling (about 30g/1oz) and shape it like a small finger, then place on a clean tray. Repeat with all the filling. By now your dough should have rested. Give it a final knead, and begin breaking off small amounts of dough (about 40g (1½oz) and rolling to form a ball. Press the ball into the palm of your hand and place a portion of date filling in the middle, then roll to encase with the dough. The date filling should be visible at each end and the middle should be encased in dough. Place on a tray lined with baking parchment and repeat until you have no more filling and dough.

Increase the oven temperature to 190°C/375°F (gas 7) and bake the shortbread for 10–15 minutes until golden. Leave to cool before handling, as they are very delicate, and dust generously with icing sugar before serving.

You can store, without the icing sugar, in an airtight container for up to 2 months.

Halawet al Jibn
Sweet Cheese

This recipe for *halawet al jibn* is my friend Majd's late uncle's. This homemade cheese differs from the store-bought version; the ratio of cheese to semolina is significantly higher, resulting in a superior dessert. If you are unable to find unsalted mozzarella, regular firm mozzarella blocks/balls work fine, although you will need to soak the cheese overnight and change the water at least 4 times. If you have access to the sweet cheese used for traditional sweets sold in many Middle Eastern grocers, that cheese is ideal.

1 quantity of sweet cream (page 208)
1 quantity of Atter (page 211)

For the sweet cheese
500g (1lb 2oz) unsalted mozzarella cheese
125ml (4fl oz/½ cup) water
250g (9oz/1⅓ cups) caster
  (superfine) sugar
60g (2oz/½ cup) coarse semolina
60g (2oz/½ cup) fine semolina
1 tbsp rosewater
1 tbsp orange blossom water
a handful of crushed pistachios,
  to garnish
a handful of rose petals, to garnish

Set aside your sweet cream before covering and transferring to the fridge. Leave the *atter* to cool and set aside.

Ensure you have a very clean and dry surface, like a kitchen work top, before you start as you will need somewhere to stretch the hot cheese dough. Have a small bowl of water handy too.

Chop up the cheese into thin slices and set aside. In a medium-sized, non-stick pan heat the water and sugar and simmer over a medium heat until all the sugar has dissolved. Turn the heat up to get it boiling, before lowering it and then adding the cheese. Using a wooden spoon, leave it to soften, stirring gently, and once the cheese has begun to melt, add the semolinas and the rose and orange blossom waters. Stir the mixture vigorously and continuously until it all comes together as a smooth cheese dough. This process takes 5–10 minutes and it also helps if you lift the dough with the wooden spoon to stretch it from the pan to see if there are any lumps of cheese that have not yet dissolved.

Working quickly, pour half a cup of the *atter* onto the clean surface and dump the cheese mixture in the middle of it. The cheese will be very hot so, using small amounts of water, rub your hands and lightly spread the cheese across the table to stretch it out as thinly as possible, reaching for more water if need be. You can also use a rolling pin for this if you would rather not touch the cheese, although the cheese does not remain hot for very long. Once you have stretched out the cheese as thinly as you can, use your fingers to lift the cheese and fan it out even further. Leave it to rest for about 20 minutes.

There are two ways to serve. Traditionally it is torn into strands and layered onto a platter, garnished with scoops of sweet cream, crushed pistachios and a generous drizzle of *atter*. Another way is to cut the large sheet of cheese into 10cm (4in) squares and placing a square in front of you on an angle so it looks like a diamond, placing a heaped teaspoon of cream in the corner closest to you and rolling it once before tucking in the sides and finally closing it. To garnish, dip one end of the cheese parcel in some *atter* and then into a bowl of crushed pistachios and rose petals.

Left and below preparing *halawet al jibn*

Halawet al Jibn comes together relatively quickly and the process is quite theatrical to watch.

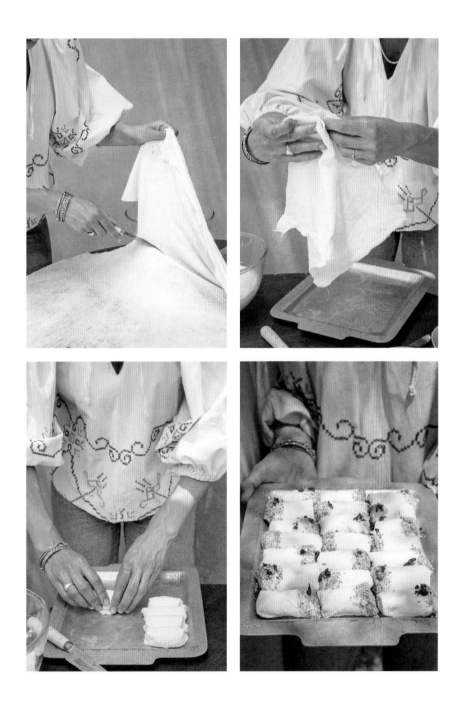

Basma
Kataifi Pastry and Sweet Cream Slice

Basma is available in Lebanese sweet shops typically during Ramadan. It reminds me of a vanilla slice, two layers of *kataifi* pastry baked in ghee until golden and crunchy, sandwiched together with a decadent sweet cream which is an ode to *ashta* (clotted cream). The elements can be made in advance and assembled on the day, which makes it the perfect entertaining dessert, especially during Ramadan after a long day of fasting.

Makes 10 discs

375g (13oz) packet of *kataifi* pastry
250ml (8½fl oz/1 cup) ghee, melted
150g (5oz/1 cup) pistachios
1 quantity of Atter (page 211)
a handful of rose petals, to garnish

For the sweet cream
250ml (8½fl oz/1 cup) milk
30g (1oz/¼ cup) fine semolina
45g (1¾oz/¼ cup) caster
  (superfine) sugar
3 tbsp double (heavy) cream
½ tbsp rosewater
½ tbsp orange blossom water
250g (9oz) fresh ricotta

To make the sweet cream, place the milk in a saucepan on a high heat and add the semolina, then whisk in the sugar and cream. Keep whisking until it starts to thicken and begins to bubble. Once it starts to bubble, keep it on the heat for a few minutes, mixing well, and add the rose and orange blossom water, stirring some more, then remove from the heat. Using a silicone spatula, fold through the ricotta and leave it to cool. Place a sheet of clingfilm (plastic wrap) over the cream to stop it from forming a skin. You can use it at room temperature or place in the fridge for the next day.

To make the pastry, preheat the oven to 180°C/350°F (gas 6).

Remove the pastry from the packet and pull it with your fingers to separate the strands and loosen it up. Fill a clean spray bottle with water and spray your pastry ever so lightly to make it easier to use and manipulate. Alternatively, you can wet your hands a few times and dampen the pastry that way.

Take a handful of the pastry, about 35g (1¼oz) and lay it out long and straight. Take one end and begin to spiral the pastry, on a flat surface, until you have made a snail shape. Lift it using a spatula and place it in a non-stick baking tray. Repeat this step with the remaining pastry (or as many as you wish to make) placing them on the baking tray, filling in any gaps you may notice in the snail with extra pastry. Lay a piece of baking parchment on top of the spirals of pastry along with a second baking tray with a weight on top to flatten the pastry into disks as flat as possible – this ensures a crispier layer when baking. After 20 minutes, remove the weight, baking parchment and tray and drizzle the ghee on top of the discs.

Bake for 30 minutes or until they reach a deep golden colour. Once you remove the tray from the oven, drain off the excess ghee into a bowl, which you can use for a second batch.

Leave the pastry layers to cool, then blitz the pistachios roughly and set aside on a plate.

To assemble, place a layer of pastry on a plate and generously top with some sweet cream and chopped pistachios, before placing a second layer of pastry on top. Garnish with dollops of the sweet cream and sprinkled crushed pistachios and serve with a generous drizzle of *atter*, and a few rose petals.

I have learnt so much about my *jido* while recreating some of his desserts. Mum recalls a milk pudding he would make, garnished with pistachios, desiccated coconut and *atter* – best of all, he called it *wahel al jannah*, which translates as 'the mud of heaven'.

Below *wahel al jannah*

Wahel al Jannah
Mud of Heaven Milk Pudding

You will need a very clean pan and wooden spoon for this dessert. I stress this because you will be able to taste any residue in the dessert.

2g (packet) of mastica
2 tsp granulated sugar
2 litres (70fl oz/8 cups) full-fat milk
300ml (10fl oz/1¼ cups) whisked double (heavy) cream
150g (5oz/1½ cups) cornflour (cornstarch)
1 tbsp rosewater
2 tbsp orange blossom water

To garnish
150g (5oz/1 cup) pistachios, crushed
75g (2½oz/1 cup) desiccated (shredded) coconut
1 quantity of Atter (right)
a handful of rose petals

Place the mastica and granulated sugar in a stainless steel mixing bowl and crush with a pestle until you have a fine sand-like consistency, then set aside. (This is a crucial step to help the mastica dissolve in the milk.)

Combine the milk, cream and cornflour in a pan, making sure there are no lumps (use a whisk) before you place it on the stove. Stir continuously on a medium heat for about 12–15 minutes until it thickens, then add the mastica and sugar mixture and the scented waters. Stir rigorously for 1 minute to combine the flavours, then remove from the heat.

Pour directly into the serving dish and, while still hot, scatter over the pistachios so they stick to the pudding and form a crust. Leave to cool to room temperature, then cover with clingfilm (plastic wrap) and place in the fridge overnight to set.

Serve cold and garnish with plenty of desiccated coconut, *atter* and rose petals.

Atter
Orange Blossom Sugar Syrup

I have several jars of this in my fridge, left over from previous desserts and ready to use for others. Treat it like maple syrup when it comes to Lebanese desserts, as it can be both an ingredient and a topping, something you can never have enough of.

Makes about 600ml (20fl oz/2½ cups)

375g (13oz/2 cups) caster (superfine) sugar
250ml (8½fl oz/1 cup) water
1½ tbsp orange blossom water
1 tbsp lemon juice

Put the sugar and water in a saucepan and bring to a boil, then simmer for 5 minutes. Add the orange blossom water and lemon juice and boil for an additional 5 minutes until the mixture begins to thicken. Remove from the heat and use according to the recipe or leave to cool before storing in an airtight jar.

Gâteau bil Chocolat wil Bascot

No-bake Chocolate Mosaic Cake

Since chocolate rarely features in traditional Lebanese sweets, this is a welcome distraction from many of the other flavours on the dessert table. I am yet to find out how this recipe made its way to the Lebanese kitchens all over the world. My version of this mosaic cake calls for roasted almonds for extra crunch, strong coffee and a generous shower of bitter cocoa when serving. Best of all it can be made a week in advance.

150ml (5fl oz/scant ⅔ cup)
   whipping cream
100g (3½oz) dark chocolate,
   roughly chopped
100g (3½oz) milk chocolate,
   roughly chopped
200g (7oz) butter
75g (21/2oz/¾ cup) cocoa
   (unsweetened chocolate) powder,
   plus extra for dusting
400g (14oz) can of condensed milk
1 shot of strong coffee
a generous pinch of salt
250g (9oz) packet of milk tea biscuits
200g (7oz/1½ cups) roasted almonds

Heat the cream in a small saucepan, removing it as soon as it starts to bubble. Add the chocolate and cover the pot for a minute to let the chocolate melt, then whisk gently until the chocolate has melted and the mixture is shiny.

Put the melted chocolate in a bowl and leave it to cool. Using the same pan, add the butter and melt it over a low heat, then mix in the cocoa powder, condensed milk, coffee and salt. Keep the heat low enough to combine the ingredients but not cook and burn them. Set the mixture aside to cool slightly.

In a large mixing bowl, break up the biscuits coarsely with your hands to resemble small broken pieces and not rubble. Add the nuts and both chocolate mixtures to the bowl and combine with a spatula. There are many ways to set this cake, either in a cake tin or loaf tin, or rolled and wrapped in parchment paper and foil and set in the freezer. If the mixture is going in a tin, line the tin with baking parchment, ensuring the top is completely covered too, then cover with a layer of foil. If you are rolling it, place it in the freezer first in the bowl for about 30 minutes for it to set slightly. You may want to split it into two logs. Line one layer of baking parchment on top of two layers of foil and put the mixture in the centre, bring up the sides to encase it like a log shape and then twist the two ends to secure them shut.

Place in the freezer for up to 6 hours, but ideally overnight.

To serve, dust generously with cocoa powder and slice into 1cm (½in) disks. Leftovers should be covered and put back into the freezer.

Mum and I often make these candied nuts (see page 214), and as the heavenly aroma fills the house, I close my eyes and find myself walking through my grandparents' little white house towards the tiny kitchen. When I open my eyes, I catch Mum chuckling to herself proudly, a fist full of candied peanuts as she tastes them, wearing my *jido*'s cheeky grin on her face. He made these nuts so often; it was his way of making peace with leaving his sweet shop behind.

Fistok Sudani bil Meleh wil Sukkar
Salted and Toffee Peanuts

Make these in batches before storing.

Makes about 500g (1lb 4oz)

For the toffee peanuts
135g (4½oz/¾ cup) caster
  (superfine) sugar
350g (12oz/2½ cups) peanuts (skin on)
a pinch of flaky sea salt (optional)

Line a tray with baking parchment and set aside. Place a medium-sized frying pan (skillet) on a high heat, add the sugar and 120ml (4fl oz/½ cup) water and, once it begins to bubble and the sugar has dissolved, add the nuts and stir continuously with a wooden spoon. After about 6 minutes the water will start to evaporate and the sugar begin to crystallize. Keep stirring continuously until the crystallized sugar begins to melt again and coat the nuts to form a toffee layer. Once the sugar has turned deep golden and all the nuts are coated, remove from the heat and pour onto the baking parchment, separating them with a fork. Sprinkle with the sea salt, if you like. Leave to cool before placing them in an airtight glass jar.

For the salted peanuts
500g (1lb 2oz/3½ cups) peanuts (skin on)
2 tbsp salt
120ml (4fl oz/½ cup) water

Preheat your oven to 180°C/350°F (gas 6) and line a baking tray with parchment.

Put the peanuts in a mixing bowl, wash well and drain. Mix the salt and water and add to the peanuts, tossing well. Tip them out onto the tray, water and all, and roast for 30 minutes, turning them every 10 minutes, so they cook evenly. Leave to cool, then store in an airtight container.

Gâteau bil Burtukal
Mum's Orange Tea Cake

There are very few Lebanese cakes, if any, yet somehow, every Lebanese mother or grandmother has a recipe for a tea cake prepared in a *bundt* tin. Mum's *bundt* cake is moist with a delicate crumb and light orange notes. Make this the night before a gathering and lightly dust it with icing sugar before serving.

Makes a 24–26cm (10–11in) round cake

a knob of butter, for greasing
300g (10½oz/2⅓ cups) plain (all-purpose)
  flour, plus extra for dusting
4 large eggs at room temperature
200g (7oz/heaped 1 cup) caster
  (superfine) sugar
1 tsp vanilla extract
200ml (7fl oz/scant 1 cup) olive oil
200ml (7fl oz/scant 1 cup) freshly
  squeezed orange juice
1–2 tbsp orange zest
3 tsp baking powder
a pinch of salt
icing (confectioners') sugar, for dusting

Preheat the oven to 170°C/340°F (gas 5). Butter and flour a 24–26cm (10–11in) bundt tin, ensuring you get into all the creases. Separate the eggs and beat the egg whites with an electric mixer until stiff peaks form, then set aside. Beat the egg yolks, sugar and vanilla until pale and fluffy, then slowly add the oil and continue beating until well combined. Add the orange juice and zest, then sift in the flour and baking powder, add the salt and, using a hand whisk, fold the flour through gently. Finally, gently fold in the egg whites until well combined. Pour the mixture into the prepared tin and bake for 50 minutes, or until a skewer comes out clean. Leave the cake to rest for 10 minutes before turning it out on a wire rack to cool. Dust with icing sugar before serving.

Mashroubat

And to Drink...

It is customary for Lebanese people to have a drink as part of their meal, making everything from fresh mint tea to traditional sparkling wines and the national spirit, *arak*, at home. With less time to prepare and increased accessibility, many of the drinks can be bought ready-made from Middle Eastern grocers.

We do, however, still make drinks like *ayran* and *lemonada* in the summer and, of course, a pot of *shai* (tea) as part of breakfast, and a *rakwet ahweh* (coffee) after a long, lazy lunch.

Ayran
Fresh Yogurt Drink

Traditionally *ayran* is made with goats' yogurt and is a popular drink prepared all over the Middle East. If you are unable to obtain goats' yogurt you can use plain yogurt; the Lebanese varieties found in the grocers are slightly sour and that is the taste you are after.

Makes about 1.3 litres (34fl oz/5 cups)

500ml (17fl oz/2 cups) goats' yogurt or
  plain yogurt
800ml (28fl oz/3½ cups) ice-cold water
sea salt, to taste
ice, to serve
mint leaves, to garnish

Place the ingredients in a blender, starting with a teaspoon of salt to taste as some yogurt varieties can be quite salty. Blitz for 30 seconds until combined. Serve in a tall glass with plenty of ice and fresh mint leaves.

Lemonada
Fresh Lemonade with Mint and Rosewater

This is one of Mum's specialities, so refreshing it transports you to a holiday at the seaside.

Makes about 2 litres (70fl oz/8 cups)

juice of 5 lemons (300ml (10fl oz/1¼ cups)
1 tbsp rosewater
185g (6½oz/1 cup) caster
  (superfine) sugar
1 bunch of mint
1.5 litres (56fl oz/6⅔ cups) water
ice, to serve
mint leaves and 1 lemon, sliced, to garnish

Squeeze the lemons and add the juice along with the remaining ingredients to a blender. Blitz to combine, ensuring the mint is very finely chopped. Serve in a tall glass with plenty of ice and garnish with fresh mint and thinly sliced lemons.

Jallab
Date and Grape Cordial with Rosewater and Pine Nuts

Jallab reminds me of Ramadan, the fridges of the grocers full of bottles of ready-made cordials such as *kharnoub* (carob drink), *toot* (mulberry drink) and *jallab*, which is a combination of date and grape molasses with hints of rose and served over ice with plenty of soaked pine nuts. Authentic *jallab*, found on street carts in Lebanon, is a deep, dark purple, and is infused with incense as part of its lengthy making process.

The aisles of the grocers also sell syrups and molasses, and although they don't come near the authentic taste, they are still very refreshing to drink. Fishing out the nuts at the bottom of the cup amongst the shaved ice is always my favourite part.

Makes about 1 litre (34fl oz/4 cups)

200ml (7fl oz/scant 1 cup) *jallab* syrup
1 tbsp rosewater
800ml (28fl oz/3½ cups) water
crushed ice
pine nuts, for sprinkling

Add the syrup, rosewater and water to a jug and stir well, pour over crushed ice and top with pine nuts.

Ahweh
Lebanese Coffee

Ahweh is synonymous with everyday Lebanese life. It is what we look forward to when we wake up in the morning and is drunk throughout the day as a visitor arrives and another leaves. Dark roast coffee can be bought at Middle Eastern grocers with or without cardamom. You will need a *rakweh* (coffee pot) and *shaffe* cups (small coffee cups) .

Makes about 4 small cups

500ml (17fl oz/2 cups) water
2 heaped tbsp ground Lebanese dark
  roast coffee
sugar, to taste

Place the water in the *rakweh* on the stove and bring to the boil. As soon as the water boils, remove from the heat, and carefully add the ground coffee one spoon at a time, stirring well. Return to the heat and watch out for an overflow.

When all the grinds are stirred in and the foamy coffee in the pot rises, lift it up and away from the heat. When the foam level settles, bring the pot closer to the heat and let the coffee foam and rise up again. Repeat the process 3–4 times until all the foam disappears.

Cover with the lid and let it settle for 3 minutes. Pour into *shaffeh* cups and serve with or without sugar, as desired.

Shai
Cinnamon and Cardamom Tea

We brew this tea in a steel tea pot and serve it in small glass cups, typically at breakfast and after a big meal, the pot constantly being topped up with more water.

Makes about 4 cups

2 heaped tbsp loose Ceylon tea leaves
1 stick of cinnamon
6 green cardamom pods
sugar, to serve (optional)

Place the ingredients in a 1-litre (34fl oz/ 4-cup) pot and fill with water. Bring to the boil, then leave it to settle for 5 minutes before serving. Pour into small glass cups and serve with or without sugar, as desired.

Shai Na'na'
Mint Tea

This soothing mint tea has subtle undertones of saffron. I often brew a small pot for myself, particularly in the cooler weather.

Makes about 4 cups

5 sprigs of mint, leaves removed
3 threads of saffron
1 tbsp caster (superfine) sugar

Place the ingredients in a 1-litre (34fl oz/ 4-cup) pot, fill with water and bring to the boil. Cover and leave to rest for 10–15 minutes. Serve in small glass tea cups.

So, What's for Dinner?

After the *sofra* has been packed away and the leftovers have been spooned into take-away containers...

Once the *ahweh* has been poured and the *shai* cups refilled, the jokes have been told and the tears have been wiped away...

Once the long goodbyes have been shared at the door, with lingering hugs full of love and gratitude for a meal filled with memories to last a lifetime...

As the sun sets, trestle tables are folded and chairs stacked high, covered with old sheets for the next time we gather...

We find our way back to the kitchen.

So, what's for dinner?

Dinner is always a plate of watermelon with mint, cheese, olives, nuts and dried fruit to cleanse the palate and end a memorable day of feasting.

Index

Acknowlededgments

Karima

First and foremost, to my marvellous mother, Sivine, you are the inspiration behind it all, it was the greatest honour to create this book with you. Thank you for not only embarking on this journey with me four years ago when we started Sunday Kitchen, but for trusting me, and for your unconditional love. This is just the beginning.

To my Abdul, you have never ever doubted me, you push me further and lift me higher.

To my daughters Layla and Eden, my only hope is that you are always proud of who you are and of your Mama.

To my sisters Susu and Amany and my best friend Terri, for always being just a phone call away.

To my dear friend Cheryl Akle, for planting the seed of belief that I should do this and for your endless flow of encouragement and wisdom.

To Jane Novak for believing in us from the very first coffee date.

To Stacey Cleworth and Claire Rochford for seeing our vision, for your patience and for giving us the space to tell our stories and share our food, thank you for creating such a beautiful book.

To the best shoot team a first-time author could ever ask for, Luisa Brimble, Ismat Awan and Jess Johnson, I will never forget the joy of those eight days together. To the generous people who gave us their homes to use for our shoots, our dear friends Barbara and Wim, the beautiful Mickey, and my dear sister-in-law Laila and to everyone who made the journey to the shoots to be part of this baby.

To my sister-in-law Hend, for all of the support on this journey and for being an excellent taste tester along the way.

To my village, there are so many of you to list, thank you for being there when I have needed you, picking me up, cheering me on and sharing stories, family recipes, and mini histories with me.

And finally, to our Sunday Kitchen community, who enter our kitchen as guests and leave as friends, you kept the dream alive.

Sivine

I never anticipated writing a cookbook, let alone collaborating with you, my beautiful daughter Karima. Your dedication and vision for this book have been truly inspiring and joyful; you never cease to amaze me.

I also want to express my heartfelt appreciation to my two daughters, Suzy and Amany, for their unwavering encouragement, love, and belief in us.

To my wonderful friends, Hend Saab, Loubna Haikal, Oula Ghannoum, and many more whose names would fill a whole page, thank you for your steadfast support during moments of frustration and doubt.

A sincere acknowledgement goes out to the entire team behind the scenes who worked tirelessly to capture the best images and layout, infused with love, care, and attention to detail.

To all the readers and home cooks who will embark on their own culinary explorations with these recipes, may each dish be a testament to the power of food to unite, heal, and delight.

Last but certainly not least, to my late mother, who taught me everything I know about flavours and spices, I wish you were here to witness what we have created. You would be immensely proud of Karima and I.

Managing Director Sarah Lavelle
Commissioning Editor Stacey Cleworth
Art Direction, Design and
Cover Illustration Claire Rochford
Photographer Luisa Brimble
Food Styling Karima Hazim Chatila
Food Preparation Ismat Awan and Sivine Tabbouch
Prop Stylist Jessica Johnson
Head of Production Stephen Lang
Production Controller Martina Georgieva

First published in 2024 by Quadrille Publishing Limited

Quadrille
52–54 Southwark Street
London SE1 1UN
quadrille.com

Text © Karima Hazim Chatila and Sivine Tabbouch 2024
Photography © Luisa Brimble 2024
Design and layout © Quadrille 2024

All rights reserved. No part of the book may be reproduced,
stored in a retrieval system, or transmitted in any form or
by any means, electronic, electrostatic, magnetic tape,
mechanical, photocopying, recording or otherwise, without
the prior permission in writing of the publisher.

The rights of Karima Hazim Chatila and Sivine Tabbouch to
be identified as the authors of this work have been asserted
by them in accordance with the copyright, Design and
Patents Act 1988.

Cataloguing in Publication Data: a catalogue record for
this book is available from the British Library.

978 1 83783 115 9

Printed in China

Karima and Sivine acknowledge the Eora
nation as the indigenous owners of the
land upon which this book was created.